CONVEYANCING 2002

CONVEYANCING 2002

KENNETH G C REID WS

Professor of Property Law in the University of Edinburgh

and

GEORGE L GRETTON WS

Lord President Reid Professor of Law in the University of Edinburgh

with a section on the Adults with Incapacity (Scotland) Act 2000
by Andrew J M Steven and Alan Barr of the University of Edinburgh

Members of the LexisNexis Group worldwide

United Kingdom	LexisNexis UK, a Division of Reed Elsevier (UK) Ltd, 4 Hill Street, EDINBURGH EH2 3JZ and Halsbury House, 35 Chancery Lane, LONDON WC2A 1EL
Argentina	LexisNexis Argentina, BUENOS AIRES
Australia	LexisNexis Butterworths, CHATSWOOD, New South Wales
Austria	LexisNexis Verlag ARD Orac GmbH & Co KG, VIENNA
Canada	LexisNexis Butterworths, MARKHAM, Ontario
Chile	LexisNexis Chile Ltda, SANTIAGO DE CHILE
Czech Republic	Nakladatelství Orac sro, PRAGUE
France	Editions du Juris-Classeur SA, PARIS
Germany	LexisNexis Deutschland GmbH, FRANKFURT, MUNSTER
Hong Kong	LexisNexis Butterworths, HONG KONG
Hungary	HVG-Orac, BUDAPEST
India	LexisNexis Butterworths, NEW DELHI
Ireland	Butterworths (Ireland) Ltd, DUBLIN
Italy	Giuffré Editore, MILAN
Malaysia	Malayan Law Journal Sdn Bhd, KUALA LUMPUR
New Zealand	LexisNexis Butterworths, WELLINGTON
Poland	Wydawnictwa Prawnicze LexisNexis, WARSAW
Singapore	LexisNexis Butterworths, SINGAPORE
South Africa	LexisNexis Butterworths, DURBAN
Switzerland	Stämpfli Verlag AG, BERNE
USA	LexisNexis, DAYTON, Ohio

© Reed Elsevier (UK) Ltd, Kenneth G C Reid and George L Gretton, 2003

All rights reserved. No part of this publication may be reproduced in any material form (including photocopying or storing it in any medium by electronic means and whether or not transiently or incidentally to some other use of this publication) without the written permission of the copyright owner except in accordance with the provisions of the Copyright, Designs and Patents Act 1988 or under the terms of a licence issued by the Copyright Licensing Agency Ltd, 90 Tottenham Court Road, London, England W1P 0LP. Applications for the copyright owner's written permission to reproduce any part of this publication should be addressed to the publisher.

Warning: The doing of an unauthorised act in relation to a copyright work may result in both a civil claim for damages and criminal prosecution.

Crown copyright material is reproduced with the permission of the Controller of HMSO and the Queen's Printer for Scotland. Any European material in this work which has been reproduced from EUR-lex, the official European Communities legislation website, is European Communities copyright.

A CIP Catalogue record for this book is available from the British Library.

ISBN 0 406 96664 8

Typeset by Waverley Typesetters, Galashiels
Printed and bound in Great Britain by Hobbs The Printers Ltd, Totton, Hampshire

Visit LexisNexis UK at www.lexisnexis.co.uk

CONTENTS

PART II : STATUTORY DEVELOPMENTS

PART III : OTHER MATERIAL

PART IV : COMMENTARY

PREFACE

This is the fourth annual survey of new developments in the law of conveyancing. As in previous years, it is divided into five parts. There is, first, a brief description of all cases reported since *Conveyancing 2001*, as well as a small number of unreported cases. The next two parts summarise, respectively, statutory developments during 2002 and other material of interest to conveyancers. The fourth part is a detailed commentary on selected issues arising from the first three parts. Finally, in Part V, there are two tables. The first, a cumulative table of appeals, is designed to facilitate moving from one annual volume to the next. The second is a table of cases digested in *Conveyancing 2001* but reported, either for the first time or in an additional series, in 2002. This is for convenience of future reference.

We do not seek to cover agricultural holdings, crofting, public sector tenancies (except the right-to-buy legislation), compulsory purchase or planning law. Otherwise our coverage is intended to be complete.

We are grateful to Professor Roddy Paisley of the University of Aberdeen and to Sheriff Douglas Cusine for providing us with the pleadings and opinions in a number of cases from the sheriff court. Our colleague Mr Alan Barr kindly allowed us to draw on his own writings on stamp duty as well as helping us in a number of other ways. We are also grateful to him and to our colleague Dr Andrew Steven for the section on the Adults with Incapacity (Scotland) Act 2000.

The text was completed on 6 February and the proofs on 16 March. As at the second date, the Land Reform (Scotland) Bill had received the Royal Assent, and the Agricultural Holdings (Scotland) Bill, the Building (Scotland) Bill, the Homelessness etc (Scotland) Bill, the Public Appointments and Public Bodies (Scotland) Bill and the Title Conditions (Scotland) Bill had completed their parliamentary stages and were awaiting Royal Assent.

Kenneth G C Reid
George L Gretton
16 March 2003

TABLE OF STATUTES

TABLE OF STATUTORY INSTRUMENTS

TABLE OF BILLS AND CONVENTIONS

Bills

Conventions

TABLE OF CASES

PART I

CASES

Note that the full text of all decisions of the Court of Session is available on the Scottish Courts website (www.scotcourts.gov.uk).

MISSIVES

(1) Spence v W & R Murray (Alford) Ltd 2002 SLT 918 (IH)

It was provided that missives should cease to be enforceable 'after a period of two years from the date of entry'. Settlement being delayed for more than two years, it was **held** that the purchaser could no longer insist on the transaction.

This affirms the decision of the sheriff reported at 2001 GWD 7-265 and digested as *Conveyancing 2001* Case (9). See **Commentary** p 55.

(2) Lonergan v W & P Food Service Ltd 2002 SLT 908, 2002 SCLR 681 (OH)

It was provided that missives should remain in effect 'notwithstanding payment of the price and delivery of the disposition but that for a period of two years'. **Held**: that the clause was void from uncertainty in that no starting date for the two-year period was stipulated; but that in any event the warranty in missives which was being founded upon would have been exempt from the time limit because of its close connection with a later agreement between the same parties. See **Commentary** p 57.

(3) Scottish Youth Theatre (Property) Ltd v Anderson 2002 SCLR 945 (OH)

It is sometimes argued, in a Continental sort of way, that parties to a contract have implied mutual duties of good faith. But in this case the duty of good faith was express, if limited in scope:

> The parties hereby agree that with effect from the date of this agreement the parties shall co-operate with one another in fairness and in good faith on all practical matters of mutual responsibility and interest affecting the implementation of the SYT [pursuers'] Project and the Trust [defenders'] Project respectively and will respond promptly to requests properly made by the other party for approvals, information or assistance.

The SYT Project was for the pursuers to acquire part of a site from the defenders and to build a complex which included rehearsal space. When the pursuers actively pursued the acquisition of a different site for the rehearsal space, the defenders intimated that they regarded the contract as repudiated, and declined to convey the site. **Held**: that, while the pursuers' conduct was disappointing to the defenders, it did not (or not yet) amount to repudiation, in respect that there had been no default, even by anticipation, in any obligation. The pursuers therefore were entitled to insist on the acquisition.

LAW OF THE TENEMENT

(4) Quantum Claims Compensation Specialists Ltd v Findlay 2002 GWD 22-733 (Sh Ct)

A case on liability for damp proofing and eradication of wet and dry rot and woodworm. See Case (17) below.

STATUTORY NOTICES

(5) Anderson v Express Investments Co Ltd 2002 GWD 28-977 (OH)

Reduction of a group of statutory notices was sought, apparently on the basis of conspiracy to injure. **Held**: that the circumstances averred—essentially that the defenders, who owned flats above and below the pursuer's flat, used access to the pursuer's flat obtained for the statutory repairs in order to carry out (private) repairs to the void between the flats—did not amount to conspiracy to injure; but that even if it did, this would not be a ground for reduction of the statutory notices.

SERVITUDES AND RIGHTS OF WAY

(6) Marshall v Duffy 2002 GWD 10-318 (OH)

Land which was the dominant tenement in a servitude of way was subsequently divided into three plots. One of the plots could only reach the servitude road by taking access across one of the other plots. **Held** (following *Bowers v Kennedy* 2000 SC 555): that the conveyance of the first plot carried with it, by implication, a right of way over the second plot.

[Another aspect of this case is digested at (23)]

(7) Thomas v Allan 2002 GWD 12-368 (Sh Ct)

Circumstances in which it was **held**: (1) that a servitude right of access 'by the existing service road' did not include the verges; (2) that a realignment of the road by the servient proprietor had been acquiesced in by the dominant proprietor and could not now be reversed; and (3) that the erection of unlocked gates, a sleeping policeman, and, at the edge, 'chicken feeder' drains and stones was within the rights of the servient proprietor and did not interfere unreasonably with the right of access.

The question of verges is often difficult, and slightly different wording can lead to different results. For earlier authorities, see *Stansfield v Findlay* 1998 SLT 784 and *Wimpey Homes Holdings Ltd v Collins* 1999 SLT (Sh Ct) 16.

(8) McNamara v Shields
2002 GWD 13-448 (OH)

A reservation of a servitude of access provided (1) that ordinary maintenance of the roads should be shared between the dominant and servient proprietors, but (2) that the cost of extraordinary damage should be met by whichever party caused it. Circumstances in which an action by the servient proprietor against the dominant for the cost of repairing extraordinary damage was **held** to have prescribed.

[Another aspect of this case is digested at (64)]

(9) Kay v Alexander
2002 SCLR 203 (Sh Ct)

Missives for the sale of a steading, which was being split off from larger subjects, provided that

> It is understood that all services are available for the proposed development but if required, you will grant necessary servitude rights to connect into any services which may be within the subjects retained by you.

Subsequently the disposition conveyed

> the water rights appertaining to the subjects hereby disponed and without prejudice to the foregoing generality those contained and referred to in [a disposition of 1971].

The pursuers, successors of the original purchasers of the steading, sought a declarator of the existence of a servitude right for the laying and maintenance of a water supply pipeline across a field belonging to the defender (the granter of the original disposition) to a water main on the public road. **Held**: action dismissed. (1) Plainly the missives did not create a servitude as such but only an obligation to grant a servitude. Therefore they did not support the declarator. In any event, the obligation in the missives was confined to services 'within' the defender's property, whereas the water main lay beyond that property. (2) The disposition referred to water rights 'appertaining' to the steading, which seemed to presuppose rights which already existed. It was hard therefore to read the disposition as creating a new servitude right. Further, the reference to the 1971 disposition was incoherent. The servitude in that case was, apparently, for the benefit of a different dominant tenement and referred to a different pipeline.

(10) Hamilton-Gray v Sherwood
Sheriff Court, 27 August 2002 (unreported)

This case, which is noted briefly in (2002) 59 *Greens Property Law Bulletin* 7, records a dispute over a servitude of aqueduct. The dominant proprietor objected to a concrete wall which was built over the pipe. The servient proprietor objected to the fact that, in at least one place, the pipe was less than three feet from the surface, contrary to the deed of servitude. It was **held** that, in the event of the pipe requiring to be reinstated, each party should be liable for one half of the cost.

(11) McMillan v Ghaly
2002 GWD 30-1046 (Sh Ct)

Construction traffic for a house, in making use of a servitude of way, trespassed beyond the point where the servitude ran and caused damage. **Held**: damages awarded but, in respect that the area covered by the servitude was unclear, interdict refused. See **Commentary** p 76.

[Another aspect of this case is digested at (62)]

(12) MacAlister v Wallace
Kilmarnock Sheriff Court, 25 June 2002, A1704/00 (unreported)

Circumstances in which a servitude of prospect/*non aedificandi* was **held** not to be breached in respect that: (1) the view under threat not being attractive, the servitude did not sufficiently benefit the dominant tenement; and (2) the building which the defender planned did not in any event fall within the area protected by the servitude. See **Commentary** p 72.

(13) Hamilton v Mundell; Hamilton v J & J Currie Ltd
Dumfries Sheriff Court, 20 November 2002, A578/01 and A591/01 (unreported)

A public road running through the defenders' land was stopped up and ceased to be public. The pursuer, who had the residual estate title, sought declarator of ownership of the road, and interdict against use by the defenders. The defenders argued: (1) that stopping up did not extinguish the public rights; (2) that the defenders' title, which derived from a split-off from the estate in 1920, included the road or at least was *habile* for the purposes of prescription; (3) that even if ownership was with the pursuer, a servitude of way was established by prescription as a result of possession during the period prior to the stopping up; and (4) (in the case of the defenders in the second action) that a right of access arose on the basis of *Bowers v Kennedy* 2000 SC 555. **Held**: the rights of the public were extinguished by the stopping up. A proof before answer would be allowed in respect of the remaining averments other than (4), in respect of which the pleadings did not disclose a relevant case.

For (3), see **Commentary** p 74. In respect of (4) the sheriff, usefully, drew attention to some of the difficulties with *Bowers v Kennedy* (right of access for landlocked property: see further *Conveyancing 2000* pp 52–54):

> Potentially difficult issues might arise as to whether the right of access can be enforced against whichever of his neighbours the party seeking access to a public road chooses; whether he must choose the least burdensome route; whether he must first seek to go through any retained land of his immediate predecessor in title if access to a public road is available through that land; or whether he must seek to go through land where access may have been exercised previously.

(14) Moray Council v Birch
Elgin Sheriff Court, 13 September 2002 (unreported)

In an action for declarator of a public right of way, the pursuer's pleadings were attacked as vague and, in places, contradictory in relation to: (1) the route of the alleged right; (2) when the prescriptive period was said to have run, and by virtue of what use; and (3) the interdict. **Held**: the challenge to (3) was well-founded, but a proof allowed in respect of (1) and (2) where the challenge, although 'interesting', failed to take account of Lord Guest's statement in *McMenemy v J Dougal & Sons Ltd* 1960 SLT (N) 84 that 'a record should not be subject to the careful and meticulous scrutiny devoted to a conveyancing deed. The matter should be looked at broadly with a view to ascertaining whether the defenders have been given fair notice of the case which the pursuer intends to prove'.

REAL BURDENS

(15) Macdonald-Haig v Gerlings
Inverness Sheriff Court, 3 December 2001 (unreported)

A right of pre-emption was created in a disposition in which the price payable was a fixed sum which, by the time of the litigation, was less than half the market value of the property. No benefited property was nominated nor was it suggested that one could be implied. **Held**: (1) the right was not contrary to article 1 of the First Protocol to the European Convention on Human Rights, notwithstanding the artificially low price; but (2) in the absence of a benefited property, the pre-emption was not a real burden and so could not be enforced in a question with successors. See **Commentary** p 63.

(16) Sheltered Housing Management Ltd v Cairns
2002 Hous LR 126 (OH)

A deed of conditions, as rectified, contained an obligation to pay a service charge of uncertain amount. The opinion was expressed, *obiter*, that such an obligation was valid as a real burden and could be enforced against successors. See **Commentary** p 66.

[Another aspect of this case is digested at (65)]

(17) Quantum Claims Compensation Specialists Ltd v Findlay 2002 GWD 22-733 (Sh Ct)

Following on from *McLay v Bennett* 1998 GWD 16-810 and *Heritage Fishings Ltd v Duke of Roxburghe* 2000 SLT 800 (discussed in *Conveyancing 1999* pp 57–59), this is further useful authority on the scope of a maintenance obligation. The obligation in question, on the upper flat in a tenement, was to pay one half of the cost of repairing, and when necessary renewing, certain parts of the building including the foundations and walls. **Held**: this was sufficient to cover the installation of a damp course in the foundations and walls (including other work incidental thereto), on the basis that that was an appropriate method of solving the problem of damp, which would otherwise affect other parts of the building. It had been argued for the upper proprietor that the work amounted to betterment and not repair, and that in any event it was for the sole benefit of the lower proprietor.

WARRANDICE

(18) Mutch v Mavisbank Properties Ltd 2002 SLT (Sh Ct) 91

A title was registered in the Land Register with the benefit of two servitudes of access. Subsequently the existence of the servitudes was challenged by the owners of the putative servient tenement, but no application was made for rectification of the Register. The purchaser sued the sellers in warrandice for £70,000. Circumstances in which **held** that there were insufficient averments as to eviction, and action dismissed. See **Commentary** p 87.

[Another aspect of this decision is digested at (24)]

COMPETITION OF TITLE

(19) Burnett's Tr v Grainger 2002 SLT 699 (IH)

The seller was sequestrated after delivery of the disposition but before its registration, some 14 months later. The trustee registered a notice of title before the disposition was registered. **Held**: that *Sharp v Thomson* 1997 SC (HL) 66 did not apply to cases of sequestration and, accordingly, that the title of the trustee in sequestration was preferred as having been registered first. See **Commentary** p 93.

This reverses the decision of the sheriff principal reported at 2000 SLT (Sh Ct) 116 (and discussed in *Conveyancing 2000* pp 93–97).

(20) Mason's Exrs v Smith
2002 SLT 1169 (OH)

In 1979 certain land at Bridgend, Crieff, was disponed to Mrs Mason by her late father's executors. The disposition was duly recorded. This land, the pursuers averred, had been in the family since the nineteenth century, the previous recorded title being in 1862. In 1979 it seems that part of the land was being tenanted by the family of the defender, with rent being paid to Mrs Mason. Eventually the rent ceased to be paid, and, in 1988, an *a non domino* disposition in respect of that part was granted to the defender by the defender's father. It too was duly recorded. The present action was at the instance of Mrs Mason's executors for the reduction of that disposition.

The case turned on whether the right held by various of Mrs Mason's forbears to complete title had been lost by negative prescription. If so, the 1979 disposition too was *a non domino* and hence no basis for the reduction of the later disposition. The applicable law was, of course, the law in force between 1617 and 1976 (when the Prescription and Limitation (Scotland) Act 1973 came into force). Unfortunately, that law was far from clear. Eventually, the Lord Ordinary (Mackay of Drumadoon) concluded that the issue had been settled by the Second Division in *Pettigrew v Harton* 1956 SC 67, to the effect that a right to complete title did prescribe negatively. Accordingly the action was dismissed.

By its nature, negative prescription can only extinguish rights. It tells us who does *not* own property, but provides no answer to the question of where ownership now lies. The answer to that can often be found in positive prescription; and indeed positive prescription, by establishing an unchallengeable right, tends to render arguments about whether negative prescription has or has not taken place irrelevant. On the present facts positive prescription was potentially of great importance. For Mrs Mason had clearly enjoyed civil possession on a *habile* title for a number of years. And, equally, the defender—at least once rent was no longer paid—had held (natural) possession on a *habile* title. Had positive prescription then run? The pursuer's attempt to argue positive prescription was rejected on the basis that it had no foundation in the pleadings. As for the defender it may be—but here we speculate—that the action had been raised before the expiry of the ten-year period, thus perhaps constituting judicial interruption of possession.

(21) Alex Brewster & Sons v Caughey
2002 GWD 15-506 (OH)

B concluded missives with A for the acquisition of land. Thereafter B (1) contracted to sell the land to C and, subsequently, (2) assigned the missives with

A to D. D then took a direct conveyance from A, which was duly registered in the Land Register. C, the disappointed first acquirer, sought reduction of the disposition from A to D as an 'offside goal' on the basis of cases such as *Rodger (Builders) Ltd v Fawdry* 1950 SC 483. In defence it was argued: (1) that the prior contract with C had been repudiated by C or had otherwise come to an end; and (2) in any event, that D did not know about the prior contract—ie was not in bad faith—until *after* taking the assignation, and such subsequent knowledge was insufficient for the rule against offside goals. **Held**: on the evidence, the prior contract had not come to an end. Further, it was sufficient for the purpose of the offside goals rule that the acquirer was in bad faith before registration, even if this was after the acquirer became bound under a contract. But in any event it was a 'questionable assumption' whether D was in good faith at the time of the assignation.

This decision is the subject of an important and wide-ranging critique by Scott Wortley, 'Double Sales and the Offside Trap: Some Thoughts on the Rule Penalising Private Knowledge of a Prior Right' 2002 *Juridical Review* 291. Wortley explores the strong similarities in this area between the laws of Scotland and South Africa, and demonstrates that, although the balance of opinion in both jurisdictions supports the view (applied in this case) that knowledge between contract and registration is sufficient for bad faith, the issue had not previously been decided. Wortley speculates as to the true legal basis of the offside goals rule and suggests that it may lie in the publicity principle. If so, it would not, in his view, support the approach taken in this case. On a different point, Wortley questions the value of reduction, except as a means of obtaining indemnity from the Keeper. For it is unclear whether the bad faith required for the reduction is equivalent to the fraud or carelessness required for rectification under s 9(3)(a)(iii) of the Land Registration (Scotland) Act 1979; and if rectification cannot take place, D would remain as registered proprietor notwithstanding the reduction of the disposition.

EXECUTION OF DEEDS

(22) Henderson's Exrs v Henderson
2003 SLT (Sh Ct) 34

Following what was averred to be an informal agreement to sell land in 1991, the seller signed, but in the event did not send, a letter to an estate agent asking him to arrange the sale. Shortly afterwards the seller died. The purchaser argued that the letter to the estate agent homologated the informal agreement, which was therefore binding on the seller's executors. It was **held** that the actings and other circumstances fell far short of what was required for homologation.

The case was, of course, decided on the law as it was before the Requirements of Writing (Scotland) Act 1995. But the result would have been the same on the current law for the more fundamental reason that s 1(5) of the 1995 Act abolishes homologation.

REGISTRATION OF TITLE

(23) Marshall v Duffy
2002 GWD 10-318 (OH)

The entry made for a servitude in the Land Register diverged to some extent from the wording of the original deed. **Held**: that, unless or until the previous wording was restored by rectification, the measure of the parties' rights was the servitude as currently expressed on the Register. See **Commentary** p 84.

[Another aspect of this case is digested at (6)]

(24) Mutch v Mavisbank Properties Ltd
2002 SLT (Sh Ct) 91

This case discusses, but does not decide, the question of whether the registered proprietor of the dominant tenement in a servitude is capable of being a 'proprietor in possession' in respect of that servitude. See **Commentary** p 85.

[Another aspect of this case is digested at (18)]

(25) M R S Hamilton Ltd v Keeper of the Registers of Scotland (No 3)
Lands Tribunal, 19 September 2001 (unreported)

A claim by M R S Hamilton Ltd for indemnity, on the ground of refusal to rectify, was admitted to proof (see 1999 SLT 829) and ultimately settled on payment of £37,500. At a subsequent hearing (1999 SLT 840) the Keeper was found liable to expenses on a party-and-party basis, ultimately taxed at £36,144.86, but reserving any claim for additional expenditure which might fall within s 13(1) of the Land Registration (Scotland) Act 1979. The current litigation concerns that additional claim. Section 13(1) obliges the Keeper to reimburse 'any expenditure reasonably and properly incurred' in a claim for indemnity. M R S Hamilton claimed £37,365.74, and, the amount having been disputed by the Keeper, appealed to the Lands Tribunal under s 25. **Held**: (1) an appeal under s 25 was competent; and (2) a realistic *prima facie* basis for the assessment of solicitors' accounts for the purposes of s 13(1) was taxation on an agent-and-client, third-party-paying basis (as opposed to an agent-and-client, client-paying basis).

RIGHT-TO-BUY LEGISLATION

(26) McAllister v Queens Cross Housing Association Ltd
2001 Hous LR 143, 2002 SLT (Lands Tr) 13

When the right to buy was first introduced (Tenants' Rights etc (Scotland) Act 1980) it applied not only to local authority landlords but also to registered housing associations. This position was continued under the Housing (Scotland) Act 1987, but was changed by the Housing (Scotland) Act 1988. However, the

1988 Act provided that those who were already tenants of registered housing associations would keep their right to buy notwithstanding the 1988 Act, which would thus apply only to new tenants. Section 43(3) provided that where a pre-1988 tenant took a new tenancy with the same housing association, the existing right to buy would apply to the property which was subject to the new tenancy. The present case was an application of that rule.

(27) Forsyth v South Ayrshire Council 2002 Hous LR 101 (Lands Tr)

The right to buy is excluded in certain types of case, one of which is sheltered housing: Housing (Scotland) Act 1987, s 61(4). In this case tenants in sheltered housing sought to compel the council to sell to them on the ground that the property did not meet the definitions in the 1987 Act. They were unsuccessful.

(28) Davidson v Dundee City Council 2002 Hous LR 104 (Lands Tr)

This case involved substantially the same facts as the previous case, and was decided in the same way.

LEASES

(29) McCallie v North Ayrshire Council 2002 SCLR 178 (Sh Ct)

A council tenant slipped on a staircase and struck a window which was at the foot, injuring herself on the glass. She sued her landlord for reparation for her injuries, founding on the Occupiers' Liability (Scotland) Act 1960. She failed. Section 2 imposes liability on occupiers. Here the occupier was the tenant, not the landlord. Section 3 imposes liability on landlords, but only where it is the landlord who has the repairing obligations, which was not the case here. In addition the defenders pled *volenti non fit injuria*. In the words of the sheriff (Colin McKay) 'The pursuer avers the danger was obvious. If so, the defenders say she accepted it by continued occupation' which had gone on for 17 years. The sheriff had some difficulty on this issue but finally decided in favour of the defenders.

Though the point was not raised in the case, if the danger was as obvious as the pursuer suggested, one wonders whether she herself, as occupier, would have been liable had a third party slipped and fallen.

The case breaks no new ground but is a useful reminder that the 1960 Act is often misunderstood in practice. For instance, it does not impose liability on the basis of ownership. Again, it imposes no absolute duty: the standard of care required by the Act is such care as is reasonable in all the circumstances of the case.

(30) PIK Facilities Ltd v Shell UK Ltd 2003 SLT 155, 2002 SCLR 832 (OH)

A commercial lease imposed various obligations on the lessee, including not only repairs but certain construction work. The landlord sought specific implement which failing damages. The lease had reached its ish and the lessee had removed from the 'demised premises' [*sic*]. **Held** (following *Sinclair v Caithness Flagstone Co Ltd* (1897) 25 R 703): that once a lease has reached its ish and the lessee has removed, specific implement is incompetent, except where the obligations in question are ones which are stated in the lease to be performed at the ish. Hence the conclusion for implement dismissed, and proof allowed on the question of damages. In addition it was said that the averments of the pursuer were 'hopelessly vague and wide'. Possibly that should have led to the dismissal of the whole case, and not only of the conclusion for implement.

(31) Paton's Trs v Caledonia North Sea Ltd 2002 GWD 16-539 (Sh Ct)

Landlords sued the former tenants for damages for the alleged deterioration of the property during the lease, and also for delivery of certain curtains said to have been removed by the tenants. The case was a fact-specific one, much depending on the construction of the terms of the lease. The defenders' attempt to have the case dismissed was unsuccessful, and proof before answer allowed. Two particular points are worth noting. The first is that the absence of an inventory was held not to be fatal to the pursuers' case, however difficult it might make matters for them at the stage of proof. The second is that one of the arguments for the defenders was that the provision in the lease whereby the tenants accepted the property as being in good order, and obliging them to maintain it, was limited to the building itself and not to moveables. On this point the sheriff (Douglas Cusine) held against them, but the point is worth bearing in mind in drafting leases.

(32) Geoffrey (Tailor) Highland Crafts Ltd v G L Attractions Ltd 2002 GWD 24-776 (Sh Ct)

An 'exclusivity clause' in a retail lease is one which bars the landlord from allowing a competing business to operate within the same retail centre. These clauses, once rare, are now common, and of considerable importance. The present case is the third such case in successive years, following on *Optical Express (Gyle) Ltd v Marks & Spencer plc* 2000 SLT 644, discussed in *Conveyancing 2000* pp 56–60, and *Miller v Clerical Medical Investment Group Ltd* 2001 SCLR 990, discussed in *Conveyancing 2001* Case (35), though the latter was rather an attempt to establish an exclusivity clause by implication—an attempt that failed. In the present case the lease in favour of the pursuers had a clause which provided that the landlords 'would not permit . . . to be used any other retail unit . . . for any purpose which includes the sale and hire of Scottish highland dress and accessories . . . [or] the sale of tartan yardage'. Despite this agreement the landlords began to sell, within the centre, dirks, broadswords and claymores, and tartan scarves, tartan ties and tartan hats. The tenants sought interdict. A proof took place, including expert evidence on such issues as what could be regarded as 'accessories' to highland dress. Interdict was granted in respect of dirks and tartan ties, but refused in respect of broadswords, claymores, tartan scarves and tartan hats. It was **held** that dirks were 'accessories' to highland dress but that broadswords and claymores were not, and that whereas tartan ties could also be regarded as accessories, tartan scarves and hats had no especially close connection with highland dress, and that 'yardage' meant simple cloth, and not ready-made garments.

(33) Countess of Cawdor v Cawdor Castle (Tourism) Ltd 2002 GWD 37-1232 (OH)

The Sixth Earl of Cawdor's marriage to his first wife, Cathryn, ended in divorce after 22 years, and was followed, in 1979, by his second marriage, to Countess Angelika von Bolowa von Chieska. When the Earl of Cawdor died in 1993 it turned out that his testament left the castle not to his eldest son, John, now the Seventh Earl, but to Angelika. Relations between the Sixth Earl's children, on the one hand, and their stepmother, now the Dowager Countess, on the other, seem to have been strained. Even before the present litigation there had been a well-publicised spat between the Dowager Countess Angelika and the Seventh Earl over GM crops, which she, as an ardent environmentalist, strongly opposed.

Many years ago the family had set up a company called Cawdor Castle (Tourism) Ltd (the defender in the present action) and the Sixth Earl had leased the castle to that company. Latterly the directors were the Seventh Earl and the two Countesses (ie the Seventh Earl's wife and stepmother), but immediately before the raising of this action the Dowager Countess resigned as director. The lease was, at least latterly, a year-to-year one terminable on six months' notice. In October 2002 the Dowager Countess served such a notice, to expire in May 2003, and she also raised an action of declarator of irritancy, on the basis of certain alleged breaches of conditions of the lease, and sought interim possession. According to media reports, what caused matters to come to a head was the fact that while the Dowager Countess was away on a visit to North America the Earl of Cawdor moved into the castle.

The lease had a conventional irritancy clause, qualified in the following manner:

> Provided that in the case of a breach, non-observance or non-performance by the tenant which is capable of being remedied, the landlord shall not exercise such option of forfeiture [*sic*] unless and until he shall first have given written notice to the tenant requiring the same to be remedied and the tenant shall have failed to remedy the same within such reasonable time as the landlord shall prescribe . . .

The court found that the defenders had indeed breached the terms of the lease but since no such notice had been given decree of irritancy would not be granted.

It is unclear why the pursuer raised the irritancy action without first giving the required notice.

(34) Peterhead Snooker Co Ltd v Strachan 2002 GWD 26-911 (Sh Ct)

After the termination of a lease the property was unavailable for re-letting because work had to be done to put the property in a state of good repair. The landlords sued the former tenants for the loss of rental income during this period. The claim failed chiefly for lack of evidence as to quantum. For an earlier stage of the case see 2001 GWD 20-777 (*Conveyancing 2001* Case (36)).

(35) Total Logistics Concepts Ltd v Argyll and Bute Council 2002 GWD 29-1024 (IH)

The local authority leased some land at Connel Airfield, near Oban, to the pursuers. The lease contained this clause:

> The said area of land shall be used by the Tenant for the purpose of the development thereon of a fuel store for the sale of aviation fuel for the users of the Airfield and for such other purposes reasonably ancillary thereto and for no other purpose whatsoever without the consent in writing of the Landlord (which consent shall not be unreasonably withheld). The Tenant shall have the exclusive right to be the sole supplier of aviation fuel at Connel Airfield for a period of Twelve years from the said date of entry hereinafter.

Despite this clause the landlords permitted aircraft users to bring in their own aviation fuel. The question for the court was purely one of interpretation of the clause: did 'supplier' have a literal meaning or did it mean only 'supplier by way of sale'? The sheriff found for the pursuers. The sheriff principal found for the defenders. The Inner House has now found for the pursuers.

(36) The Hoy Trust v Thomson 2003 SLT (Sh Ct) 20

In general an action to remove a tenant must be by way of a summary cause. In this case the landlords proceeded, not by way of a summary cause, but by way of a summary application. **Held**: that the action was incompetent. The sheriff principal (Sir Stephen Young) referred to s 35(1) of the Sheriff Courts (Scotland) Act 1971, and continued:

> The present action is a civil proceeding in the sheriff court, it is an action for the recovery of possession of heritable property, and there is no additional or alternative claim. It follows in my opinion that it should have been raised as a summary cause and that it was not competent to have raised it as a summary application. I do not think that s 21(4) of the [Agricultural Holdings (Scotland) Act] 1991 . . . undermines this conclusion. As I understood her, the respondents' solicitor read this sub-section as meaning that the provisions of the [Sheriff Courts (Scotland) Act] 1907 . . . relating to removings should have effect in the case of an agricultural holding with the result

> that the pursuers were entitled to rely upon s 36 of that Act. But this is not what s 21(4) says. Section 36 of the 1907 Act remains in force in any event, and all that s 21(4) of the 1991 Act does is to provide that, in the case of an agricultural holding, s 36 should have effect subject to s 21 of the 1991 Act . . . The form of application for a summary warrant of ejection in terms of s 36 of the 1907 Act is not there specified and, whatever may have been the position before the 1971 Act came into force, it is in my opinion plain in light of s 35(1)(c) that an application such as has been made by the pursuers in this case which is not accompanied by a crave for any other type of remedy must be made in the form of a summary cause. Indeed rule 30.3 of the Summary Cause Rules 2002[1] (which is the successor to rule 69 of the Summary Cause Rules 1976[2] . . .) specifically provides that, when decree for the recovery of possession of heritable property is granted, it shall have the same force and effect as '(c) a summary warrant of ejection' in terms of s 36 of the 1907 Act.

(37) Glasgow City Council v Morrison Developments Ltd 2003 SLT 263 (OH)

Landlords of commercial premises raised an action of declarator of irritancy on the grounds that a grassum had not been timeously paid. Since the date when the grassum should have been paid was more than five years previously the defenders pled prescription. It was held that the obligation to pay the grassum was an 'obligation relating to land' and so subject to the 20-year prescription: Prescription and Limitation (Scotland) Act 1973, Sch 1, para 1(2)(e). Accordingly decree was granted in favour of the pursuers.

(38) Cavriani v Robinson 2002 Hous LR 67 (Sh Ct)

A property was let under a short assured tenancy. It was for 12 months from 18 August 1997, and it was provided that it would continue thereafter from the 18th of each month to the 18th of the next, until terminated by the landlord on giving 28 days' notice. The landlord gave notice on 16 September 1999 to terminate the tenancy with effect from 18 November 1999. When the tenant did not remove the landlord raised an action, founding on s 33 of the Housing (Scotland) Act 1988, which requires the tenant of a short assured tenancy to remove at the agreed ish, provided certain preconditions are met. The tenant argued, in the alternative: (1) that on 18 August 1998 the tenancy had been renewed for 12 months by tacit relocation, and that the same had happened on 18 August 1999, so that the next ish would be 18 August 2000; or (2) that if the month-to-month renewal provision was effectual, then that meant that the tenancy had ceased to be a short assured tenancy (since a short assured tenancy must be for at least six months), with the consequence that the tenant was not bound to remove.

1 Act of Sederunt (Summary Cause Rules) 2002 (SSI 2002/132) Schedule (Summary Cause Rules).
2 Act of Sederunt (Summary Cause Rules, Sheriff Court) 1976 (SI 1976/476) Schedule (Summary Cause Rules).

Both arguments failed, and decree was pronounced in favour of the pursuer. The winning argument for the pursuer was based on s 32(3) of the 1988 Act which provides that:

> If at the ish of a short assured tenancy (a) it is continued by tacit relocation or (b) a new contractual tenancy . . . comes into being . . . the continued tenancy or, as the case may be, the new contractual tenancy shall be a short assured tenancy, whether or not it fulfils the conditions of a short assured tenancy.

Arguably, however, s 32(3) was inapplicable. As for (b) there was no '*new* contractual tenancy' since the defender continued in possession under the *existing* contract. For the same reason (a) seems inapplicable, since 'tacit relocation' means an *implied* ('tacit') agreement to continue an existing lease beyond its originally-agreed ish, whereas this lease continued after 18 August 1998 by its own *express* terms. In short, 18 August 1997 was not, it seems, the ish, and so s 32 was, it may be argued, inapplicable. On this view the only ish was 18 November 1999; and the lease whose ish happened on 18 November 1999 was, we suggest, a short assured tenancy by virtue of its original creation, and not by virtue of the savings in s 32. However, on the facts of the case the point did not matter.

It is noteworthy that the tenancy agreement provided for a notice period of 28 days, but in fact the notice period given was just over two months. One imagines that the pursuer had regard to s 33(2) of the 1988 Act which provides that a landlord who wishes to bring a short assured tenancy to an end must, two months in advance, serve on the tenant a notice 'stating that he requires possession'. It is unclear whether such a notice is or is not the same as a notice to quit: in practice it obviously makes sense to have a single notice which is, on any view, both a notice to quit and a s 33(2) notice. (See further Angus McAllister, *Scottish Law of Leases* (3rd edn, 2002) p 401.)

(39) Mackenzie v Aberdeen City Council
Aberdeen Sheriff Court, 20 June 2002 (unreported)

This case, which is noted briefly at (2002) 59 *Greens Property Law Bulletin* 6, was an action for damages against the landlords for alleged poisoning by carbon monoxide fumes. **Held**: that any liability of the landlords could only be fault-based and not strict.

(40) Robb v Dundee District Council
2002 SC 301, 2002 SLT 853 (IH)

Damp public-sector housing has been an issue for many years. There has even been a book on the subject: Paul D Brown, *Dampness and the Law: the Law in Scotland on Dampness and Disrepair in Public and Private Rented Housing* (1987). Dampness has prompted a good deal of litigation by tenants against their landlords. Claims have been litigated in a variety of ways. (For two other examples see below.) In the present case the argument was that the damp was a 'nuisance' within the meaning of the Environmental Protection Act 1990, ss 79 and 82. The pursuer was unsuccessful before the sheriff and appealed to the sheriff principal. Her appeal failed. She then appealed again, also unsuccessfully. The view taken by the court was that the building itself, though imperfect, was not below minimal standards. The damp was condensing damp, not rising damp or penetrating damp. If heated in a normal way the property would not have been damp. The damp was thus caused not by defects in the building but by the fact that it was inadequately heated. In short, the real cause of the dampness was not the building but the pursuer's poverty.

(41) McGuire v Glasgow District Council
2002 Hous LR 134 (Sh Ct)

This case, though reported in 2002, was decided in 1983. The essential facts were much as in *Robb* (above), but the claim was a common law one, not a statutory one. The decision was much the same as in *Robb*, namely that the damp was not rising damp or penetrating damp, but condensing damp, and that the real problem was not that the building was defective but rather that the tenant was not heating it properly.

(42) Edinburgh District Council v Davis
2002 Hous LR 136 (Sh Ct)

This case, though reported in 2002, was decided in 1984. A council property suffered severely from damp, and the tenants sued their landlords for damages at common law. The damp was of two sorts. One was penetrating damp, caused by flooding in the neighbouring property, which was a vacant council house that was constantly attacked by vandals, who broke pipes and thus caused flooding. The other type of damp was condensing. There was no rising damp. The story, vividly told by Sheriff N E D Thomson, is heartbreaking. He found the Council liable in damages for both kinds of damp. Whether the Council should have been liable for the condensing damp is, however, open to some doubt: see the previous two cases.

(43) Scott v Thomson
2003 SLT 99, 2002 Hous LR 144 (IH)

A landlord who unlawfully evicts a tenant is liable in damages at common law. But there are also statutory provisions. Section 22, as amended, of the Rent (Scotland) Act 1984 provides that unlawful eviction can constitute an offence. And s 36 of the Housing (Scotland) Act 1988 provides that:

> If . . . a landlord or any person acting on his behalf unlawfully deprives a residential occupier of any premises of his occupation . . . the landlord shall . . . be liable to pay the former residential occupier . . . damages assessed on the basis set out in s 37 . . .

(Although a 'residential occupier' will in the normal case be a tenant, the meaning of the term in the 1988 Act is quite broad.) Section 37 says that the quantum of damages is the difference between the value of the property with vacant possession and the value which the property would have had as occupied. The idea is to take away from the landlord any gain which would otherwise be achieved by the unlawful eviction. How much the damages will amount to will vary considerably according to the circumstances of the case: for instance if a short assured tenant is unlawfully evicted the damages under ss 36 and 37 would presumably be slight or even zero.

Mr and Mrs Thomson owned a house in Dunoon which was let to the pursuer. The Thomsons' son had management powers and he unlawfully evicted the pursuer, by changing the locks while she was on holiday. She sued her landlords for damages based on ss 36 and 37 of the 1998 Act, and obtained decree from the sheriff for £33,000 plus interest plus expenses. The defenders appealed to the sheriff principal, who reversed. The pursuer appealed to the Court of Session, which reinstated the decision of the sheriff. The central issue in the case concerned the meaning of the phrase 'or any person acting on his behalf'.

(44) TCS Holdings Ltd v Ashtead Plant Hire Co Ltd
2003 SLT 177 (OH)

A lessee sued a neighbouring lessee (both holding from the same landlord) for damage done, or alleged to have been done, by reason of the latter's fault, to a drainage pipe serving the pursuer's leased land and running through the defender's leased land. **Held**: that the pursuer did not have sufficient title to sue, and action dismissed. (For analysis of this area of law, see K G C Reid, *The Law of Property in Scotland* para 126.)

TRUSTS, LIFERENTS AND TAILZIES

(45) Stronach's Exrs v Robertson
2002 SLT 1044, 2002 SCLR 843 (IH)

Held: that where property is being neglected by a proper liferenter, the fiar's remedy is to require that the liferenter find caution, known as liferent caution (*cautio usufructuaria*). See **Commentary** p 79.

(46) Earl of Balfour Ptr
2002 SLT 981 (IH) *rev* 2002 SLT 1385 (HL)

A case on liferents and quasi-entails which turned on whether, for the purposes of ss 47 and 48 of the Entail Amendment (Scotland) Act 1848, the date of a deed of trust meant the date of the deed as originally executed or the date of a subsequent codicil. See **Commentary** p 82.

(47) Brodie v Secretary of State for Scotland 2002 GWD 20-698 (OH)

A case arising out of a sale by trustees allegedly in breach of trust. See **Commentary** p 78.

(48) Armstrong v G Dunlop & Sons' Judicial Factor 2003 GWD 2-37 (OH)

This is the latest round in a long dispute. (See also *Armstrong Ptr* 1988 SLT 255, *G Dunlop & Sons' Judicial Factor v Armstrong* 1994 SLT 199 and *G Dunlop & Sons' Judicial Factor v Armstrong* 1995 SLT 645.) Mr and Mrs Dunlop were the partners of a farming partnership, Messrs G Dunlop & Sons. They became estranged about 1982. In 1986 Mr Dunlop petitioned for the dissolution of the partnership and for the appointment of a judicial factor to the partnership assets, and an interlocutor to that effect was pronounced in 1987. Soon afterwards the parties were divorced, and it was agreed that a farmhouse with garden ground should be conveyed to Mrs Dunlop. For reasons that are unclear this never happened, but it seems that Mrs Dunlop did, over the years, live in the property in question. The judicial factor wished to sell the property. In 1994 he obtained an interdict to stop Mrs Dunlop interfering in the sale of the property, but no sale seems ever to have occurred. In 2001 he obtained decree against her in the sheriff court for recovery of possession. In the present action Mrs Dunlop sought reduction of that decree, interim interdict against its enforcement, and declarator that she was entitled to receive from the judicial factor a disposition of the property. Her reason for reduction was that she had been in ill health and had thus been unable to give proper instructions. The Lord Ordinary granted interim interdict in favour of the pursuer.

The facts behind the case are evidently complex and unhappy. Although only a decision on interim interdict, and thus not finally disposing of the issues, the opinion of the Lord Ordinary has much of interest, on the questions such as the reduction and suspension of sheriff court decrees, and on trust law.

As the Lord Ordinary (Drummond Young) observes:

> it is a general principle of trust law that beneficiaries of full legal capacity who are entitled to the fee of trust estate may at any time compel trustees to make over the trust property to them: *Miller's Trs v Miller* (1890) 18 R 301; *Yuill's Trs v Thomson* (1902) 4 F 815.

Given that the partnership had been dissolved, the beneficial interest in the farm assets was *prima facie* vested in Mr and Mrs Dunlop as individuals. If it was the case that they had agreed that a particular part of the assets in question should be conveyed to Mrs Dunlop, and if that agreement was still valid and binding, then, since the judicial factor was in the position of a trustee, it would *prima facie* follow that the judicial factor was bound to give effect to the agreement, provided, of course, that there was no other legitimate reason why he should not do so. At all events, that was a sufficiently cogent argument to support interdict on an interim basis.

STANDARD SECURITIES AND FLOATING CHARGES

(49) Davidson v Clydesdale Bank plc
2002 SLT 1088 (OH)

A heritable creditor who enforces by sale is under an obligation to achieve the best price reasonably obtainable. This is a common law rule and is also set forth expressly in s 25 of the Conveyancing and Feudal Reform (Scotland) Act 1970: 'It shall be the duty of the creditor to advertise the sale and to take all reasonable steps to ensure that the price at which all or any of the subjects are sold is the best that can be reasonably obtained.' In the present action the Clydesdale Bank enforced a standard security by sale. In 1993 the debtor raised an action against the bank for damages of £2,500,000, alleging that the bank had sold at below a fair value. For reasons that are unclear the case did not come to proof until 2002. The specific complaint was that the property (Ardlethen Farm, near Ellon) had large reserves of gravel and sand which were capable of commercial exploitation, but the property had been marketed without sufficiently drawing this fact to the attention of potential purchasers. The action failed, after proof, on the ground that the price achieved had in fact been a fair value.

(50) Clydesdale Bank plc v Black
2002 SLT 764, 2002 SCLR 857 (IH)

An important case on cautionary wives, considering the application to Scotland of the decision of the House of Lords in the English appeal, *Royal Bank of Scotland plc v Etridge (No 2)* [2001] 4 All ER 449. See **Commentary** p 60.

(51) Thomson v Royal Bank of Scotland
2002 GWD 18-591 and 2002 GWD 23-744 (OH)

A husband and wife granted a standard security over the family home, to secure the indebtedness of a company, Thomas Loudon Ltd, of which the husband was a director. The wife sought reduction, apparently of the entire standard security. (It is unclear on what basis she sought reduction of the security *quoad* her husband's share.) She averred that she had signed as a result of her husband's undue influence, and that the defenders had not acted in good faith. The debate took place largely on the basis of *Royal Bank of Scotland plc v Etridge (No 2)* [2001] 4 All ER 449, but soon after the debate the Inner House decision in *Clydesdale Bank plc v Black* (see above) was issued, as a result of which parties were invited to make further submissions. A proof before answer was allowed.

(52) Clydesdale Bank plc v McCaw
2002 GWD 18-603 (IH)

This case raises some interesting questions about the enforcement of standard securities in the context of sequestration. See **Commentary** p 57.

(53) Abbey National v Briggs
Glasgow Sheriff Court, 20 June 2002 (unreported)

This is the first case known to us applying the Mortgage Rights (Scotland) Act 2001. Details can be found on the website of Govan Law Centre (www.govanlc.com). For a discussion of the 2001 Act, see *Conveyancing 2001* pp 75–84.

The defender craved the court to 'grant an order in terms of s 2 of the Mortgage Rights (Scotland) Act 2001 to continue the cause for six months to allow the payment of mortgage arrears to be made at the rate of £6 per fortnight and for payment of the defender's monthly mortgage payment with effect from 28 August 2002 and to suspend the pursuer's rights of enforcement of the standard security which arose on default for twelve months from the date of the order'. The defender gave evidence and also led evidence from his doctor and from the local manager for the 'Shelter' charity on the question of the reasonable availability of alternative accommodation. (Section 2 of the 2001 Act provides that one of the factors to be taken into account by the court is 'the ability of the applicant and any other person residing at the security subjects to secure reasonable alternative accommodation'.) Abbey National led no evidence and were prepared to consent, subject to a payment schedule of £18 per fortnight rather than £6. The sheriff (Kenneth Mitchell) granted the order in the terms sought by the defender.

(54) Clydesdale Bank plc v Hyland
2002 GWD 37-1229 (Sh Ct)

Heritable creditors sought decree for possession. **Held**: that the action was regulated by s 5 of the Heritable Securities (Scotland) Act 1894 and accordingly was subject to the new rule 3.3(3) of the Ordinary Cause Rules.

(55) Bank of Ireland v Morton (No 2)
2002 GWD 38-1244 (IH)

This case has a complex history, arising out of the insolvency of a company called Lewis Lloyd Holdings Ltd (LLHL).

LLHL granted two floating charges, one to the Royal Bank of Scotland plc and the other to Bass Brewers Ltd. Later the company wished to buy a certain property and the Bank of Ireland agreed to advance £250,000 for this purpose. The letter offering the loan, addressed to Brian Morton as managing director of LLHL, required that there be:

(i) first standard security over the freehold [*sic*] site known as the Hazelburn Business Park, Campbeltown, comprising offices, workshop and cleared site to the rear;

(ii) personal guarantee from Brian Morton for the sum of £250,000.

The loan was made, the property purchased with it, and at the same time the standard security and the guarantee were granted. Later the company got into financial problems and went into receivership. The receivers sold the property for £150,000. There were, however, considerable problems about how the Bank of Ireland, the Royal Bank of Scotland and Bass Brewers Ltd should rank. These problems led to two litigations. In the first, *Griffith and Powdrill (Receivers of Lewis Lloyd Holdings Ltd) Ptrs* 1998 GWD 40-2037, it was held that in terms of the documentation the standard security was postponed to the two floating charges. Nothing dismayed, Bank of Ireland returned to the attack. Although this might be the correct interpretation of the effect of the documentation, it was not, they argued, the real intention of the parties, at any rate as far as the Bass charge was concerned. The real intention of the various parties, they argued, was that the standard security should rank ahead of the Bass charge. Accordingly they sought judicial rectification of the documentation in terms of s 8 of the Law Reform (Miscellaneous Provisions) (Scotland) Act 1985. In this they were successful: *Bank of Ireland v Bass Brewers Ltd* 2000 GWD 28-1077. (See *Conveyancing 2000* Cases (56) and (74) and pp 81–83 and 117–119.) But this litigation seems to have been limited to the Bass charge, with the Royal Bank charge unaffected.

What has happened to the £150,000 for which the property was sold is unclear. Bank of Ireland achieved priority over Bass by virtue of the outcome of the rectification action. But Bass have, or are said to have, priority over Royal Bank by virtue of a ranking agreement, while at the same time Royal Bank appear to have priority over Bank of Ireland. In other words, there seems to be a priority circle.

Meanwhile, the Bank of Ireland were also seeking to enforce Mr Morton's guarantee against him. When he did not pay they raised the present action, which has now reached the Inner House. (For an earlier stage of the present action see *Conveyancing 2000* Case (55).) The defender's position was that he had signed the guarantee on the basis that the Bank would obtain a first-ranked standard security, that their failure to obtain a first-ranked standard security was their fault, and that accordingly he should be released from his cautionary liability to the extent that he was prejudiced by their failure. Of course, if the £150,000 is still subject to unresolved priority issues, the extent to which the defender was prejudiced remains unclear. Had the court sustained the defender's argument, difficult issues of quantification would thus have arisen. As the court says (para 24):

> the extent of any loss to the defender is wholly uncertain. It cannot be determined on the basis of the evidence before the sheriff. Senior counsel for the defender made it clear that he did not know the true position as between the pursuers and the floating charge holders, or for that matter the extent of any loss which the pursuers themselves had sustained.

The Inner House held that the guarantee was enforceable in full. The terms of the guarantee signed by the defender were such as to preclude any defence based on the terms of the offer of loan made to LLHL, even if the defender could assert rights under that offer. For instance, clause R of the guarantee provided that 'this guarantee shall not be discharged nor shall the guarantors' liability be affected by reason of any failure or irregularity, defect or informality in any security given by or on behalf of the customer . . .'.

The defender's best authority was *Fleming v Thomson* (1826) 2 W & S 277, where a creditor failed to complete title to a heritable security and for that reason was held to be barred from enforcing against certain cautioners. But in that case the obligation to take heritable security was part of the contract of guarantee itself.

The court held, as a matter of fact, that 'the defender would not have signed the guarantee had he thought that the pursuers would not get a first-ranking security. The reason there was no ranking agreement was fault on the part of the pursuers' agents' (para 25). In these circumstances it is difficult not to feel sympathy for the defender. One wonders whether the defender might not try to do what the pursuers themselves did: seek judicial rectification. It might be argued that the original agreement between the pursuers and the defender was that the pursuers would obtain a first-ranking security, and if the terms of the guarantee failed to reflect that agreement, then the position must be put right by judicial rectification. That may seem a stretch, but it is perhaps no more of a stretch than the rectification successfully obtained by the pursuers against Bass.

If the defender were to pay in full under the guarantee, he would then presumably be entitled to an assignation from the pursuers of all their rights based on the standard security: this is the *beneficium cedendarum actionum*. Thus if (1) the defender pays in full and if (2) it turns out that the Bank of Ireland did have first ranking on the £150,000, then (3) the defender would receive that sum (subject to any adjustments on account of expenses, interest etc), with the result that (4) the defender at the end of the day would seem to be in the same position as he would have been had he won the present action.

SOLICITORS AND ESTATE AGENTS

(56) Guardian Investments Ltd v Iain Smith & Co 2002 GWD 8-264 (Sh Ct)

Guardian Investments Ltd sued two firms of solicitors, I and B. The sheriff exercised his discretion to require the pursuers to find caution for any expenses that might be awarded against them. (This power is conferred by s 726 of the Companies Act 1985 and can be exercised where the court considers it unlikely that a litigant that is a company would be able to pay expenses.) The pursuers appealed to the sheriff principal on a number of grounds, one being that their case was a strong one and it would be unjust to defeat it by requiring caution to be found, and another being that an order for caution would contravene the pursuers' human rights, and in particular Article 6 of the ECHR which confers the right to a fair trial. The appeal was dismissed.

As averred by the pursuers, the story was that they had concluded missives to buy property to develop it, using I as their solicitors, but financial problems prevented them from going ahead with the deal. They then moved from I to another firm, B. They withdrew from the missives, and another company, A, which was said to be controlled by partners of I, and which used I as their solicitors, proceeded to buy the property and develop it. The pursuers felt aggrieved at these alleged events and considered that I had breached their fiduciary duties to them.

On the basis of the brief report it is not possible to assess the strength of the pursuers' argument based on fiduciary duty. It is true that fiduciaries, such as trustees, agents, or company directors, must not make use of their position to make a profit for themselves. The rule is best-developed in company law, where such English decisions as *Regal (Hastings) Ltd v Gulliver* [1967] 2 AC 134 and *Industrial Developments Consultants Ltd v Cooley* [1972] 2 All ER 163 come to mind. But the rule is so rooted in the doctrines of English equity that it is often difficult to know precisely what the position in Scotland is. In practice, this is an area in which English authorities are used rather indiscriminately.

(57) Adams v Thorntons
2002 SCLR 787 (OH)

The pursuer entered into a complex property transaction which went wrong. He alleged that his solicitors had been negligent and claimed damages against them. They pled that, *esto* they had been negligent, the claim had prescribed negatively. This is often a key issue in professional negligence claims. In such actions the prescription defence is often met, by the pursuer, with s 11(3) of the Prescription and Limitation (Scotland) Act 1973, which says that if the claimant was excusably unaware of the 'loss injury or damage' then the prescriptive clock does not begin to tick until s/he was so aware, or should reasonably have become so aware. The pursuer here duly pled s 11(3), and also s 6(4), under which the starting of the clock is delayed if the claimant's delay was by reason of error induced by the other party. Proof before answer was allowed.

(58) Royal Bank of Scotland plc v Macbeth Currie
2002 SLT (Sh Ct) 128

A familiar story: a lender suing a firm of solicitors for alleged negligence. The case turns on the law of positive prescription: see Case (63).

(59) Cheltenham & Gloucester plc v Sun Alliance and London Insurance plc (No 2)
2002 GWD 18-605 (OH)

A case in which the insurers under the Master Policy successfully denied liability. See **Commentary** p 68.

(60) Wylie v Jeffrey Aitken
2002 GWD 40-1360 (OH)

Circumstances in which the pursuer failed to prove that a purchase on unsatisfactory terms as to sewage was at the behest of his solicitor. See **Commentary** p 70.

BOUNDARY DISPUTES/PRESCRIPTION

(61) Caledonian Heritable Ltd v Canyon Investments Ltd (No 2)
2002 GWD 5-149 (IH)

A debate on a technical point of pleading, centering on whether a particular averment should be admitted for probation. The Lord Ordinary had disallowed the averment: see 2001 GWD 1-62 (*Conveyancing 2000* Case (69)). An Extra Division now admitted it.

(62) McMillan v Ghaly
2002 GWD 30-1046 (Sh Ct)

Circumstances in which damages were awarded for trespass, in respect both of physical damage and of distress and inconvenience.

[Another aspect of this case is digested at (11)]

(63) Royal Bank of Scotland plc v Macbeth Currie
2002 SLT (Sh Ct) 128

A disposition was granted which, it was argued, was *a non domino*. Nonetheless the grantee lived in the house for six years until ejected, following a court action, by the Royal Bank, who were heritable creditors. Thereafter the bank had control of the house, although it was not let for two years. **Held**: the alleged defect in the disposition may have been cured by positive prescription. In particular, (1) the action by the bank did not constitute judicial interruption; (2) the possession of the bank could be treated as the civil possession of the grantee; and (3) although the property was vacant for two years, the fact that the bank was in control during that period meant that it was still being possessed. Proof before answer allowed.

(64) McNamara v Shields
2002 GWD 13-448 (OH)

A disposition reserved a servitude of way subject to an obligation to pay for any extraordinary damage to the road. More than five years after the alleged damage occurred, the owner of the road sued for payment. **Held** (following *Lord Advocate v Shipbreaking Industries Ltd* 1991 SLT 840): that this was an obligation to make reparation rather than an obligation relating to land. Hence it prescribed after five years and could no longer be enforced. Further, even if the saving in Sch 1, para 2(c) to the Prescription and Limitation (Scotland) Act 1973 for obligations constituted by a probative writ survived the repeal of that provision by the Requirements of Writing (Scotland) Act 1995 so far as concerns pre-1995 writs (which was doubted), the obligation to pay for damage arose in part out of the acts complained of and could not be said to be constituted by a probative writ.

[Another aspect of this case is digested at (8)]

RECTIFICATION AND REDUCTION

(65) Sheltered Housing Management Ltd v Cairns 2002 Hous LR 126 (OH)

A deed of conditions for a sheltered housing complex omitted, by mistake, the clause imposing an obligation to pay a service charge. The managers/superiors sought to have the deed rectified by insertion of the clause. Some owners objected, arguing, under s 9 of the Law Reform (Miscellaneous Provisions) (Scotland) Act 1985, that they had bought their properties in reliance on the unrectified deed. **Held**: rectification allowed. The evidence was that the owners had no specific knowledge of the content of the deed of conditions and so could not be said to have relied thereon. See **Commentary** p 98.

[Another aspect of this case is digested at (16)]

(66) Co-operative Wholesale Society Ltd v Ravenseft Properties Ltd 2002 SCLR 644 (OH)

The Co-op were Ravenseft's tenants in a shopping centre in Dundee. It was averred that the parties agreed to delete the keep-open clause of the lease, and a minute of variation was entered into accordingly. But while this deleted the principal keep-open clause, it failed to delete clause 10.16 in terms of which the tenants obliged themselves:

> To keep the premises open for retail trade during the usual hours of business in the locality . . . the shop display windows being kept dressed in a suitable manner and in keeping with a good class shopping centre.

Later Ravenseft sold their interest to Douglas Shelf Seven Ltd (DSSL), and when the premises were not duly kept open in terms of clause 10.16 DSSL raised an action of damages for £70,000. The Co-op responded by seeking rectification of the minute of agreement to the effect of deleting clause 10.16 as (or so they argued) had always been the intention. DSSL pled s 9 of the Law Reform (Miscellaneous Provisions) (Scotland) Act 1985. They had bought in reliance on the minute of agreement in its original form, and rectification would be prejudicial to their position. At an earlier hearing, noted at 2001 GWD 24-905 (*Conveyancing 2001* Case (80)), averments in support of this argument were held relevant and proof before answer was allowed. At this hearing the relevance of averments by the Co-op was considered.

The Co-op sought to prove that the continuing presence of clause 10.16 would, in the face of the minute of agreement, have aroused the suspicions of any experienced purchaser (such as DSSL). Thus insofar as DSSL relied on the unrectified minute, (1) they were in bad faith, or (2) at any rate their reliance was unreasonable (1985 Act, s 9(3)). **Held**: proof before answer allowed. It was not an objection to (2) that it relied on the same factual basis as (1). See **Commentary** p 99. **Also held** relevant for probation was an averment that, in a rent review, the figure fixed by the arbiter would have been the same whether clause 10.6 was present or not. To call the arbiter as witness on a hypothetical question did not disturb the principle that an arbiter cannot be asked to explain his decision.

MATRIMONIAL HOMES ACT

(67) Stevenson v Roy
2002 SLT 445 (OH)

This was an action to enforce occupancy rights against purchasers from the husband. The pursuer alleged that she had been ejected by force from the matrimonial home, Nylow (formerly Rubislaw), King O' Muirs Road, Glenochil, Tullibody, Clackmannanshire, in 1993 and that her husband—who was the sole owner—had sold the property to the defenders in 1995. She raised the present action against the buyers in 1998. It seems that when the defenders purchased the property in 1995 they obtained the usual affidavit from the seller, but the action was fought out on another issue: prescription.

Section 6(3) of the Matrimonial Homes (Family Protection) (Scotland) Act 1981, as amended, provides that occupancy rights prescribe if 'the entitled spouse has permanently ceased to be entitled to occupy the matrimonial home, and at any time thereafter a continuous period of 5 years has elapsed during which the non-entitled spouse has not occupied the matrimonial home'. Mr Stevenson sold the house in 1995, so the five-year period began to run then. It had not elapsed by the time the pursuer raised the action in 1998 but it had elapsed by 2002 when the debate took place. (Why it took so long is unclear.) The rule for prescription under the general law, contained in the Prescription and Limitation (Scotland) Act 1973, is that the raising of the action interrupts the running of the prescription: if that was so in this case the defence of prescription would fail. However, it was held that in relation to occupancy rights under the 1981 Act the raising of an action does not interrupt prescription, and accordingly the action was dismissed.

DILIGENCE AND INSOLVENCY

(68) Karl Construction Ltd v Palisade Properties plc
2002 SC 270, 2002 SLT 312 (OH)

This case **held** that an inhibition on the dependence should be recalled as violating the defender's ECHR rights. The decision has created much stir, and there have been several other cases in its wake, such as *Advocate General for Scotland v Taylor* 2002 GWD 23-740 (OH), *Dunalastair Investments Ltd v Young* 2002 GWD 4-123 (OH), *Barry D Trentham Ltd v Lawfield Investments Ltd* 2002 SC 410, 2002 SLT 1094 (OH), *Fab-Tek Engineering Ltd v Carillion Construction Ltd* 2002 SLT (Sh Ct) 113 and *Irving's Curator Bonis v Skillen* 2002 SLT (Sh Ct) 119. See further 2002 SLT (News) 119.

RESIDENTIAL CARE FOR THE ELDERLY

(69) Robertson v Fife Council
2002 SLT 951, 2002 Hous LR 78 (HL)

The central issue was whether a local authority can refuse to provide residential care to someone who needs it, on the grounds that the person's means are above the applicable threshold, or whether it must provide the care and then seek to recover the cost, an attempt which may be in vain if the person has in fact disposed of his or her assets. In practice what will have happened is that the main asset is a house that has been transferred to some other member of the family, and if the local authority could refuse care that would pressurise the family into finding the resources. The House of Lords, reversing the Court of Session (reported at 2001 SLT 708), has now **held** that the local authority must provide the care first and then seek to recover.

For previous discussions, see *Conveyancing 2000* pp 120–123 and *Conveyancing 2001* pp 34–35. And see also the comments of Alastair Bissett-Johnson and Shona Main at 2002 SLT (News) 279 and Ken Swinton at (2002) 70 *Scottish Law Gazette* 143.

The Community Care and Health (Scotland) Act 2002 now changes the landscape, introducing the principle of 'free personal care'.

PART II

STATUTORY DEVELOPMENTS

Note that the text of all Acts and statutory instruments, both of Scotland and of the United Kingdom, is available on www.hmso.gov.uk.

PROTECTION OF WILD MAMMALS (SCOTLAND) ACT 2002 (asp 6)

Section 1 of this controversial Act, which is aimed chiefly at foxhunting, provides that '[a] person who deliberately hunts a wild mammal with a dog commits an offence'. The Act came into force on 1 August 2002: see The Protection of Wild Mammals (Scotland) Act 2002 (Commencement) Order 2002 (SSI 2002/181). An attempt to strike it down by judicial review failed: *Adams Ptr* 2002 SCLR 881.

FINANCE ACT 2002 (c 23)

Section 92 of the Finance Act 2001 (together with the Variation of Stamp Duties Regulations 2001 (SI 2001/3746)) introduced a stamp duty exemption for land in disadvantaged areas. In Scotland such areas are defined by postcode, and a complete list is given on pp 41–43 of *Conveyancing 2001*. As originally enacted, the exemption applied to conveyance on sale duty and duty paid on lease premiums but only where the consideration (or premium) was less than £150,000. Section 110 of the Finance Act 2002 (which inserts new ss 92A and 92B into the 2001 Act) now provides the legislative framework for an extension of this exemption. In due course regulations will be introduced raising the threshold of £150,000 in the case of non-residential property only. At present the extent of the likely increase is unclear and depends on EU approval for what would otherwise be state aid. The new s 92B contains a detailed definition of 'residential property'.

Among the other changes made to stamp duty in Part 4 of the 2002 Act are the following:

- Stamp duty is no longer payable on transfers of goodwill in respect of instruments executed on or after 23 April 2002 (s 116). This is part of a longer-term strategy to confine conveyance on sale duty to land and shares.
- Contracts for the sale of land with a consideration in excess of £10 million now attract conveyance on sale duty, unless the conveyance is presented for stamping within 90 days (s 115). This anti-avoidance provision strikes at contracts which, in the English phrase, are 'resting on contract'. Its impact in Scotland is likely to be small.
- Penalties for late stamping of deeds executed outside the UK are to run from 30 days after the date of execution rather than, as previously, from 30 days after the documents were brought into the UK (s 114).
- Sections 111–113 qualify or remove exemptions concerned with transfers within a group of companies and some other matters.

ENTERPRISE ACT 2002 (c 40)

This prospectively abolishes receivership, at least in ordinary cases. See **Commentary** p 89.

PROCEEDS OF CRIME ACT 2002 (c 29)

This is of tangential interest to conveyancers. It sets up a new confiscation regime, with a new Assets Recovery Agency. It also updates and consolidates the criminal law relating to money laundering.

COMMONHOLD AND LEASEHOLD REFORM ACT 2002 (c 15)

This has nothing to do with Scots law. It introduces 'commonhold' to English law. It will apply mainly to blocks of flats. We mention it mainly because English clients (including English lenders) may now start asking whether Scottish tenements are 'commonhold'.

LAND REGISTRATION ACT 2002 (c 9)

This too has nothing to do with Scots law. It is a major reform of the English law, and we mention it because English clients might ask about it.

THE HOUSING (SCOTLAND) ACT 2001 (COMMENCEMENT NO 6 AND AMENDMENT) ORDER 2002 (SSI 2002/433)

A substantial number of provisions of the Housing (Scotland) Act 2001 were brought into force during 2002. The explanatory note to this, the final commencement order of the year, lists the provisions now in force together with the commencement dates.

ACT OF SEDERUNT (AMENDMENT OF ORDINARY CAUSE RULES AND SUMMARY APPLICATIONS, STATUTORY APPLICATIONS AND APPEALS ETC RULES) (APPLICATIONS UNDER THE MORTGAGE RIGHTS (SCOTLAND) ACT 2001) 2002 (SSI 2002/7)

This amends the Ordinary Cause Rules[1] and Summary Applications Rules[2] in the sheriff court to make provision for actions falling within ss 1(1)(b) or 1(1)(c) of the Mortgage Rights (Scotland) Act 2001 (respectively applications by heritable creditors under s 24 of the Conveyancing and Feudal Reform (Scotland) Act 1970 and under s 5 of the Heritable Securities (Scotland) Act 1894). Provision is also made for applications for orders under s 2 of the Act. The changes are discussed by Anthony F Deutsch at (2002) 45 *Greens Civil Practice Bulletin* 3. For an account of the Mortgage Rights Act itself, see *Conveyancing 2001* pp 75–84.

THE CIVIC GOVERNMENT (SCOTLAND) ACT 1982 (LICENSING OF HOUSES IN MULTIPLE OCCUPATION) AMENDMENT ORDER 2002 (SSI 2002/161)

The Civic Government (Scotland) Act 1982, s 44(1)(b) provides that, in addition to the various types of activity that the Act expressly requires to be licensed, statutory instruments can be made bringing in new types of activity. Landlords who wish to let out dwellinghouses by way of multiple occupancy require permission in terms of the Civic Government (Scotland) Act 1982 (Licensing of Houses in Multiple Occupation) Order 2000 (SSI/2000/177). The latest order makes minor changes.

THE LAND REGISTRATION (SCOTLAND) ACT 1979 (COMMENCEMENT NO 16) ORDER 2002 (SSI 2002/432)

With effect from 1 April 2003 this Order extends registration of title to all remaining parts of Scotland, ie to the counties of Banff, Moray, Ross and Cromarty, Caithness, Sutherland, and Orkney and Shetland.

COMMENCEMENT OF PART 6 OF THE ADULTS WITH INCAPACITY (SCOTLAND) ACT 2000 (asp 4)

Part 6 of this Act came into force on 1 April 2002. Conveyancing is affected in particular by ss 56 and 61 which relate to the registration in the Land or Sasine Registers of, respectively, intervention orders and guardianship orders. See **Commentary** p 100.

---

1 Sheriff Courts (Scotland) Act 1907, Sch 1 (Ordinary Cause Rules 1993).

2 Act of Sederunt (Summary Applications, Statutory Applications and Appeals etc Rules) 1999 (SI 1999/929).

PART III

OTHER MATERIAL

TITLE CONDITIONS (SCOTLAND) BILL

This far-reaching Bill, of the first importance to conveyancers, was introduced to the Scottish Parliament on 6 June 2002 and is expected to complete its parliamentary stages in the first months of 2003. Most of it is not due to come into force until 28 November 2004, the day on which the feudal system is to be abolished (see below).

'Title conditions' means real burdens, servitudes, conditions in long leases, and one or two other obligations. But the bulk of the Bill is concerned with real burdens. Part 1 codifies the common law but with a number of changes. In future any deed can be used to create real burdens, but it must nominate the benefited property as well as the burdened, and must be registered against both properties.

A simple new procedure ('termination') is introduced for the extinction of burdens which are more than 100 years old (with some exceptions). The person affected by the burden serves and registers a notice and, unless a person with enforcement rights applies to the Lands Tribunal for renewal, the burden is extinguished. Part 1 of the Bill also reduces the period of negative prescription from 20 years to 5, and contains a provision on acquiescence.

Part 2 introduces the idea of 'community burdens'—burdens which are reciprocally enforceable within a housing estate, or tenement, or other grouping of properties. This is a new name for burdens which have been commonplace for many years. Part 2 provides for majority decision-making in relation to the carrying out of common maintenance and the appointment and dismissal of a manager. There are simplified (although not simple) rules for variation and discharge. Generally this requires the consent either of a majority of owners, or of all owners within four metres (not counting roads).

Conservation burdens and maritime burdens are already familiar from the Abolition of Feudal Tenure etc (Scotland) Act 2000. Part 3 of the Bill allows such burdens to be created in the future. These are real burdens in favour of a person, and there is no benefited property. But in each case the person is restricted. A conservation burden may only be created in favour of a conservation body and

Scottish Ministers, and a maritime burden in favour of the Crown. Under the Bill, Scottish Ministers and local authorities can also be holders of a new type of burden, known as an economic development burden. As its name suggests, this is a burden with the purpose of promoting economic development.

Part 4 abolishes all existing *implied* rights of enforcement of real burdens, and provides new implied rules in their place. At the time of writing these include a rule that, where burdens are imposed under a common scheme on a group of properties, the owner of each property has mutual enforcement rights. A typical example would be a housing estate subject to a single deed of conditions. This rule has, however, proved controversial, and it is possible that it will not survive. All the rules on implied rights are, more or less, confined to burdens imposed by a deed registered before 28 November 2004. For new burdens it will, as already mentioned, be necessary to nominate the benefited property or properties, and there can be no question of enforcement rights arising by implication.

Not all of the Bill concerns real burdens. Part 6 introduces a model management scheme, suitable for larger developments, and known as the Development Management Scheme. The residents' association is a body corporate (although not a company), and provision is made for annual budgeting, sinking funds, annual meetings and so on. Part 7 makes a number of alterations to the law of servitudes, including the abandonment, in the case of registered servitudes only, of the rule that servitudes must be of a type already recognised by the law. Part 8 concerns pre-emptions, and also reversions under the School Sites Act 1841. Part 9 introduces new rules, both procedural and substantive, in relation to discharge of title conditions by the Lands Tribunal. Finally, Part 10 covers a wide variety of miscellaneous topics, including the extinction of real burdens and servitudes on compulsory purchase.

LAND REFORM (SCOTLAND) BILL

This Bill was introduced on 27 November 2001 and, at the time of writing, was awaiting royal assent. The Bill as introduced is summarised at pp 47–49 of *Conveyancing 2001*.

AGRICULTURAL HOLDINGS (SCOTLAND) BILL

This Bill was introduced on 16 September 2002. As and when enacted, it will make major changes to the law of agricultural tenancies. The Bill proceeds on the assumption that the current system of agricultural holdings (regulated by the Agricultural Holdings (Scotland) Act 1991) has made owners of farmland reluctant to let the land, and has also given rise to the evasion of the legislation by the use of limited partnerships. Hence the Bill proposes that tenancies created in the future will be subject to a regime that is more even-handed as between landlord and tenant. There will be two new types of agricultural tenancy, namely the limited duration tenancy (up to 15 years) and the short limited duration tenancy (up to 5 years). Tenant farmers are given a statutory pre-emption right, the price to be set by a complex system of valuation.

BUILDING (SCOTLAND) BILL

This Bill was introduced on 18 September 2002. Building law is currently governed by the Building (Scotland) Act 1959, as amended. The new Bill will repeal the 1959 Act, but the basic ideas will remain in place. There will still be a system of building warrants and completion certificates, and details of building standards will still be found in regulations rather than in primary legislation. So whilst this Bill, as and when enacted, will bring about considerable changes it will, so to speak, build on existing foundations. One important change for conveyancers is the intended replacement of letters of comfort by 'building standards assessments' carried out by the local authority (s 6). A potential, but presumably unavoidable, difficulty is that these will assess buildings by reference to the current regulations. For a review of the Bill, see an article by A D Anderson published at (2002) 70 *Scottish Law Gazette* 172.

PUBLIC APPOINTMENTS AND PUBLIC BODIES ETC (SCOTLAND) BILL

For the most part this Bill has nothing to do with conveyancing. However, the Bill contains provisions to abolish the Scottish Conveyancing and Executry Services Board (s 4), transferring the Board's regulatory powers to the Law Society of Scotland (s 12). Licensed conveyancers ('independent conveyancing practitioners') are given certain powers of notaries public when the need arises in the course of conveyancing services (s 14). The Bill was introduced on 17 June 2002.

SALMON AND FRESHWATER FISHERIES (CONSOLIDATION) (SCOTLAND) BILL

This Bill, introduced to the Scottish Parliament on 27 November 2002, consolidates the mass of legislation relating to salmon and freshwater fisheries, including the Salmon and Freshwater Fisheries (Protection) (Scotland) Act 1951 and the Freshwater and Salmon Fisheries (Scotland) Act 1976. It implements a Report by the Scottish Law Commission on *Consolidation of Certain Enactments Relating to Salmon and Freshwater Fisheries in Scotland* (Scot Law Com no 188, 2002; available on www.scotlawcom.gov.uk).

HOMELESSNESS ETC (SCOTLAND) BILL

This, as and when enacted, will make certain changes to the Housing (Scotland) Act 1987.

ABOLITION OF THE FEUDAL SYSTEM

On 21 November 2002 the Deputy First Minister, Mr Jim Wallace, announced in Parliament that the 'appointed day' for the abolition of the feudal system will be Martinmas (28 November) 2004. A statutory instrument is required under s 71 of the Abolition of Feudal Tenure etc (Scotland) Act 2000. Assuming that this is duly made, the feudal system will be abolished on 28 November 2004. The Title Conditions (Scotland) Bill (see above) will come into force on that day. Mr Wallace also indicated that Part 4 of the 2000 Act—which allows superiors to preserve burdens, or alternatively to claim compensation, by registration of a notice—is intended to be commenced in the autumn of 2003. All notices must be registered before the appointed day.

BARONY TITLES AND ARMORIAL BEARINGS

Section 63 of the Abolition of Feudal Tenure etc (Scotland) Act 2000 will, on the appointed day, sever the connection between barony titles and land but preserve the titles themselves, including any associated heraldic privilege. The following statement has been issued by the Lord Lyon King of Arms (2003 SLT (News) 6):

> In connection with the appointed day under the above Act, which has been announced to be 28 November 2004, the following rules will apply:
>
> 1. With effect from the appointed day the Lord Lyon will no longer officially recognise a person as a feudal baron, nor make any grant of baronial additaments as part of armorial bearings.
>
> 2. Any petition for recognition as a baron and/or for baronial additaments must be submitted to the Court of the Lord Lyon not later than 30 April 2004 in order to allow time for it to be processed before the appointed day. No such petition lodged after 30 April 2004 will be considered.
>
> 3. After the appointed day the Lord Lyon will be prepared to consider allowing a blue chapeau as part of the arms matriculated by an heir of a baron who has been recognised by the Lord Lyon prior to the appointed day, in a similar manner as blue chapeaux have in the past been, and will continue to be, allowed to representers of former owners of baronial lands.
>
> 4. After the appointed day a baron who has a grant of arms with baronial additaments may continue to use the additaments for his lifetime. Use of the additaments by his heirs after the death of the baron will not be permissible and all existing grants will be subject to this rule.

LETTERS OF OBLIGATION: 21 DAYS FOR REGISTRATION

As from 1 November 2002 the period for registration of the acquirer's deed permissible in 'classic' letters of obligation has been extended from 14 days to 21 days. This is in acknowledgment of delays at the Stamp Office and the Registers. Solicitors are still enjoined to register as soon as possible.

A 'classic' letter of obligation enjoys preferential status under the Master Policy. There is no excess, and claims are disregarded for discounting/loading purposes in respect of future premiums. In a note in the *Journal of the Law Society of Scotland* for October 2002 Lionel Most summarises the qualifying conditions of such a letter in the following way:

> For a letter of obligation to be treated as 'classic', it must be restricted to standard undertakings only—these comprise covering the 'gap' period in the search and obliging the granting solicitor to deliver, as appropriate, a discharge and/or a feuduty redemption receipt . . . In addition, there are four requisites as follows:
>
> 1. A search must have been carried out 'immediately prior to settlement' including in Sasine cases a search in the computerised presentment book and the search must be clear. [The Council of Mortgage Lenders require a search to be dated no more than three days prior to the date of entry. Such a search would presumably qualify as 'immediately prior to settlement'.]
>
> 2. Proper enquiry must have been made of the client regarding any outstanding security or other matter which might adversely affect the search.
>
> 3. The granter of the letter of obligation must be unaware of any other security or other matter which might adversely affect the search.
>
> 4. The granter of the letter of obligation must have (control of) sufficient funds to pay the loan and/or the redemption of feuduty as the case may be (and must know the identity and whereabouts of the party entitled to the redemption money).

REGISTRATION OF RIGHTS IN SECURITY BY COMPANIES

In October 2002 the Scottish Law Commission published a *Discussion Paper on Registration of Rights in Security by Companies* (Scot Law Com DP no 121, available on www.scotlawcom.gov.uk). One of its main proposals is that, in future, only floating charges should be registrable at Companies House, thus bringing to an end the double registration of standard securities. See **Commentary** p 91.

COMMUNICATIONS WITH PROPERTY MANAGERS

Some points arising out of a meeting between representatives of the Conveyancing Committee of the Law Society and the Property Managers Association Scotland Limited are summarised in the *Journal of the Law Society of Scotland* for February 2002 (p 33). Enquiries are often made of property managers by solicitors acting for purchasers. The Association's advice to its members is that they should respond only on the following matters:

- confirmation that *cumulo* feuduty has been paid or exhibition of the *cumulo* feuduty receipt;
- confirmation whether there are any arrears of common charges in respect of the property being sold;

- details of the common insurance policy (a copy of the policy to be produced only if payment is made for copying charges); and
- details of any repairs which have been instructed by the manager but not yet carried out.

Thus, for example, a manager cannot guarantee that common repairs are not in contemplation, for he cannot know what is in the minds of the owners.

It is necessary to inform managers of the sale and of the name of the new owner. The apportionment of the common charges may take time, since most firms now issue quarterly accounts, and it is important that the seller's solicitor retains sufficient funds to cover the likely cost.

CML LENDERS' HANDBOOK FOR SCOTLAND

A second edition has been prepared and came into effect on 1 January 2003. It is only available electronically (on www.cml.org.uk/handbook). Only a small number of changes have been made since the first edition (for which see *Conveyancing 2000* pp 83–86 and *Conveyancing 2001* p 53). One is to require that property enquiry certificates include questions on entries in the Contaminated Land Registers (which local authorities have been under a duty to maintain since 14 July 2000). Other changes are listed on p 10 of the *Journal of the Law Society of Scotland* for September 2002. For a discussion, see an article by Ken Swinton published at (2002) 70 *Scottish Law Gazette* 173.

FSA REGULATION OF MORTGAGE ADVICE

The Financial Services Authority (www.fsa.gov.uk) has announced that it will be extending the scope of regulation to certain types of mortgage. According to the press release (www.fsa.gov.uk/pubs/press/2002/084.html):

> The following activities will be regulated: mortgage lending; mortgage administration; advising on a regulated mortgage contract; and arranging a regulated mortgage contract. Firms that will need authorisation include banks, building societies, specialist lenders and mortgage intermediaries.

According to the FSA paper (www.fsa.gov.uk/pubs/cp/cp146.pdf):

> Any solicitor . . . who carries on the activities of advising on or arranging mortgages in the course of his profession (which doesn't consist of regulated activities) is excluded from the regulated activities of arranging or advising on mortgages.

It is expected that the rules will be promulgated in 2003 and come into force in 2004.

REFORM OF THE LAW OF DILIGENCE

Provisional proposals for reform of the law of diligence, including heritable diligence, were published by the Scottish Executive in April 2002. See *Enforcement of Civil Obligations in Scotland: a Consultation Document* (available on www.

scotland.gsi.gov.uk/consultations/justice/CivOb-00.asp). Comments were invited by 16 July 2002. This cycle of law reform is separate from the replacement of poindings, which has now been effected by the Debt Arrangement and Attachment (Scotland) Act 2002. The aspects of the paper of interest to conveyancers are as follows.

(1) As to inhibitions, the Executive proposes to adopt the proposals of the Scottish Law Commission's *Report on Diligence*, published in 2001 (Scot Law Com no 183; available on www.scotlawcom.gov.uk). Under these proposals inhibitions will survive, but subject to certain changes.

(2) As to adjudication, the Executive again proposes to adopt the proposals of the Scottish Law Commission's *Report on Diligence*. Under these proposals adjudication would be abolished and replaced by a new diligence called land attachment. One noteworthy feature of the Executive's paper is that whereas the Law Commission deliberately left open the question of whether dwelling-houses could be sold under the new procedure, the Executive has now expressly said that the sale of dwellinghouses will be competent, albeit subject to certain safeguards.

(3) There is a discussion of sequestration for rent, and the possibility of abolition is canvassed. The discussion is perhaps not as well thought-through as it might be, and the implications of abolition have not been fully considered. There is a valuable article by Andrew Steven, 'Goodbye to the Landlord's Hypothec?' 2002 SLT (News) 177.

(4) The Executive proposes to abolish the action of maills and duties, as being irrelevant in modern law. However, here too it may be that the analysis is not deep enough. An action of maills and duties is the procedure whereby a heritable creditor can recover rents from tenants in the security subjects. When the standard security was introduced in 1970 this action continued in practice but the name 'maills and duties' was dropped, because some argued that the remedy under a standard security is not an 'action of maills and duties'. It would be unfortunate were the law of standard securities to be changed unintentionally, as a result of a muddle about terminology.

(5) There are certain proposals for modifying the procedures used in removings and ejections.

HOUSING IMPROVEMENT TASK FORCE

The Housing Improvement Task Force was set up by the Scottish Executive in December 2000. Its remit focuses on three main areas:

- houses and flats in need of repair in the owner-occupied sector;
- buying and selling of houses; and
- renting property in the private sector.

The first stage of the Task Force's work was to consider the legal, administrative and financial elements under current arrangements and to assess their effects. This stage was completed with the publication, in March 2002, of the Task Force's *Issues in Improving Quality in Private Housing*. The second and final stage, which will make recommendations for action, is expected to be completed in March 2003. The stage 1 report and other materials are available from the Task Force's website (www.scotland.gov.uk/hitf).

Of particular interest to conveyancers is the Task Force's work in its second area (buying and selling of houses), which may lead to a recommendation for the introduction of sellers' packs and sellers' surveys. The issues here are discussed by Ken Swinton at (2002) 70 *Scottish Law Gazette* 69 and by Linsey Lewin at (2002) 47 *Journal of the Law Society of Scotland* Aug/21. Work in the first area (repair in the owner-occupied sector) may impact to some extent on the Tenements (Scotland) Bill, which is expected to be introduced in the next parliament.

REGISTERS OF SCOTLAND

Customer contact points

A diagram showing the appropriate person to contact for different types of inquiry in relation to the Land Register and Register of Sasines was published on p 9 of the *Journal of the Law Society of Scotland* for March 2002. This gives names, telephone numbers and email addresses.

Registration of discharges

An account of Land Register practice in relation to discharges of standard securities is given on pp 30–31 of the *Journal of the Law Society of Scotland* for April 2002. Worked examples cover registration at different points in the conveyancing cycle, and there is guidance as to fees and documents to be submitted.

Natural water boundaries

Following discussion in the Joint Consultative Committee of the Registers of Scotland and the Law Society of Scotland, the Keeper's practice in relation to natural water boundaries has changed. (See p 11 of the *Journal of the Law Society of Scotland* for May 2002.) In respect of applications made on or after 20 May 2002 the Keeper will (1) show the maximum extent of the water boundary within the title plan, but (2) exclude indemnity in respect of the movement of the boundary feature (eg by alluvion or avulsion). The practice applies to any boundary which comprises the foreshore or a natural water feature (river, loch or the sea). This replaces the practice set out at paras 6.99 ff of the *Registration of Title Practice Book*.

Standard securities by companies

Section 410 of the Companies Act 1985 requires a standard security to be registered in the Register of Charges within 21 days of its registration in the Land/Sasine Register. The application to the latter should be marked at the top with 'Confirmation of Registration is required', preferably in red letters. (See p 32 of the *Journal of the Law Society of Scotland* for July 2002.) The Keeper will then confirm the date of registration free of charge. As the confirmation indicates, applicants should forward a copy of the Certificate of Registration of Charge to the Keeper as soon as available. If this is not done within 60 days the charge certificate will exclude indemnity in respect of possible failure to register in the Register of Charges. It will then be for the applicant to seek restoration of indemnity on production of the Certificate.

CARBETH (AND OTHER) HUTTERS

On 15 December 2000 the Scottish Executive issued a paper seeking views on whether statutory protection should be introduced for Carbeth (and other) hutters. A 'hutter' is a person who has the use of a hut which has been built or acquired primarily as a holiday or weekend home. The land itself is leased, usually from year to year and at a low rent. Research suggests that there are around 600 huts in Scotland on some 27 sites. The largest and most prominent site is at Carbeth, near Blanefield in Stirlingshire, which has around 170 huts. Most huts date from the 1930s.

On 7 November 2002 Mr Jim Wallace, the Deputy First Minister, gave the following answer to a parliamentary question about the Executive's proposals following consultation:

> Consideration of the consultative response has confirmed substantial drawbacks to any attempt to legislate in this area. Legislation would be contrary to the fundamental principles of Scots law, in particular that leased land under a short lease reverts to the landlord at expiry of the lease and that property built on leased land belongs to the landlord; legislation could not be retrospective or applicable to hutters only, and its promotion might precipitate changes to the ownership and management of comparable estates in Scotland which would be profoundly damaging to the interests of hutters. We are aware that constructive discussions continue at local level to resolve the difficulties at Carbeth. It would not be appropriate for the Executive to seek to intervene in private negotiations between landlord and tenants, but we would encourage local resolution of such difficulties.

CRU REPORT ON HOUSE BUYING AND SELLING

In 2002 the Scottish Executive Central Research Unit published a report, *House Buying and Selling in Scotland*, carried out on its behalf by DTZ Pieda Consulting and NFO System Three. Selected findings are that:

- 76% of buyers were successful with their first offer.

- 66% of surveys/valuations were Scheme 1.
- Many buyers were unclear about the differences between the different possible types of survey/valuation.
- 'It took people an average of 14 weeks from starting to look seriously for a house to making a successful offer. There was wide variation, with 21% taking less than three weeks and 14% taking longer than 31 weeks. The average total time, from starting to look seriously to date of entry was 23 weeks.'
- As for sellers, 'in 45% of cases an offer was accepted within a month. One fifth of sales took more than three months before an offer was accepted'.
- As for solicitors, 'there was not much support for standardising missives to reduce delays'.

BOOKS

FRASER R BARRACLOUGH, *A Practical Guide to Rent Review of Agricultural Holdings in Scotland* (W Green/Sweet & Maxwell, 2002; ISBN 0 414 01506 1)

A BOYLE, C HIMSWORTH, A LOUX and H MACQUEEN (eds), *Human Rights and Scots Law* (Hart, 2002; ISBN 1 841113 044 3) (which includes a chapter by George Gretton on property law)

DAVID W COCKBURN, *Commercial Leases* (Butterworths, 2002; ISBN 0 406 94712 0)

D J CUSINE and ROBERT RENNIE, *Standard Securities* (2nd edn) (Butterworths, 2002; ISBN 0 406 93914 4)

MARK HIGGINS, *Scottish Repossessions: The Mortgage Rights (Scotland) Act 2001* (W Green, 2002; ISBN 0 414 01465 0)

ANGUS MCALLISTER, *Scottish Law of Leases* (3rd edn) (Butterworths 2002; ISBN 0 406 93238 7)

M C MESTON, *Succession (Scotland) Act 1964* (5th edn) (W Green 2002; ISBN 0 414 01453 7)

COLIN T REID, *Nature Conservation Law* (2nd edn) (W Green/Sweet & Maxwell, 2002; ISBN 0 414 01355 7)

KENNETH REID and GEORGE GRETTON, *Conveyancing 2001* (Butterworths, 2002; ISBN 0 406 95703 7)

JOHN H SINCLAIR, *Legal Drafting in Scotland* (W Green/Sweet & Maxwell, 2001; ISBN 0 414 01284 4)

JOHN H SINCLAIR, *Handbook of Conveyancing Practice in Scotland* (4th edn) (Butterworths, 2002; ISBN 0 406 95705 3)

DAVID M WALKER, *Prescription and Limitation of Actions* (6th edn) (W Green 2002; ISBN 0 414 01460 X)

ARTICLES

A D ANDERSON, 'The End of Letters of Comfort' (2002) 70 *Scottish Law Gazette* 172

ALASTAIR BISSETT-JOHNSON and SHONA MAIN, 'The Community Care and Health (Scotland) Act 2002 and *Robertson v Fife Council*' 2002 SLT (News) 279

STEWART BRYMER, 'Reform of Irritancy in Leases of Land' (2002) 57 *Greens Property Law Bulletin* 1

STEWART BRYMER, '20 Things You Really Need to Know About Leasing Commercial Property' (2002) 47 *Journal of the Law Society of Scotland* July/7

STEWART BRYMER, 'E-Conveyancing—The Future Here Today?' (2002) 58 *Greens Property Law Bulletin* 5

STEWART BRYMER, 'Code of Practice for Commercial Leases' (2002) 59 *Greens Property Law Bulletin* 1

STEWART BRYMER and SCOTT WORTLEY, 'Preparing Superiors for Feudal Abolition' (2002) 60 *Greens Property Law Bulletin* 6 and 61 *Greens Property Law Bulletin* 1

DAVID CABRELLI, 'Negative Pledges and Ranking Reconsidered' (2002) 7 *Scottish Law & Practice Quarterly* 18 (commenting on *Bank of Ireland v Bass Brewers Ltd* 2000 GWD 28-1077)

DAVID CABRELLI, 'When is the Refusal of Consent by Landlord or Tenant Unreasonable?' (2002) 7 *Scottish Law & Practice Quarterly* 117

DAVID CABRELLI, 'Commercial Leases: When is the Refusal of Consent by a Landlord or Tenant Unreasonable?' (2002) 58 *Greens Property Law Bulletin* 3

RAFFAELE CATERINA, 'A Comparative Overview of the Fair Wear and Tear Exception: the Duty of Temporary Interests to Preserve Property' (2002) 6 *Edinburgh Law Review* 85

JAMES CHALMERS, 'In Defence of the Trusting Conveyancer' 2002 SLT (News) 231 (on the use of the trust clauses in the context of *Sharp v Thomson*)

DOUGLAS J CUSINE, 'Local Authority Consents and the Authority as Superior' 2002 *Scottish Planning and Environmental Law* 82

ANTHONY F DEUTSCH, 'Circumventing the Mortgage Rights (Scotland) Act 2001' (2002) 43 *Greens Civil Practice Bulletin* 1

ANTHONY F DEUTSCH, 'Practical Aspects of Litigation Arising out of the Mortgage Rights (Scotland) Act 2000' (2002) 45 *Greens Civil Practice Bulletin* 3

Isobel D'Inverno, 'Stamp Duty—Budget 2002 Changes' (2002) 57 *Greens Property Law Bulletin* 5

Lord Eassie, 'Reforming Registration of Company Charges' (2002) 47 *Journal of the Law Society of Scotland* Dec/26

George L Gretton, 'Registration of Company Charges' (2002) 6 *Edinburgh Law Review* 146

David Guild, 'The Registration of Rights in Security by Companies' 2002 SLT (News) 289

Brent Haywood, 'A Lack of Diligence' (2002) 47 *Journal of the Law Society of Scotland* Oct/28 (commenting on *Karl Construction Ltd v Palisade Properties plc* 2002 SC 270)

Mark Higgins, 'Serving Notices under the Mortgage Rights Act' (2002) 47 *Journal of the Law Society of Scotland* May/22

Mark Higgins, 'A Break from the Old Routine: The Doctrine in *Smith*' 2002 SLT (News) 173

Linsey Lewin, 'Scottish Executive Housing Improvement Task Force' (2002) 47 *Journal of the Law Society of Scotland* Feb/32 and Aug/21

Linsey Lewin and Stewart Brymer, 'Builders' Missives: The Case for Standardisation' (2002) 60 *Greens Property Law Bulletin* 1

Linsey Lewin and Stewart Brymer, 'Scottish Executive Housing Improvement Task Force' (2002) 58 *Greens Property Law Bulletin* 1

Linsey Lewin, 'Automated Registration of Title to Land' (2002) 47 *Journal of the Law Society of Scotland* Nov/25

David Logan and Scott Blair, 'Inhibitions on the Dependence: An Alternative View' 2002 SLT (News) 119

Angus McAllister, 'Long Residential Leases—Some Unfinished Business' (2002) 7 *Scottish Law & Practice Quarterly* 141

A J McDonald, 'Rectification and Indemnity in the Land Register' (2001) 55 *Greens Property Law Bulletin* 6 and (2002) 56 *Greens Property Law Bulletin* 1

Derek J McGlashan, 'Udal Law and Coastal Land Ownership' 2002 *Juridical Review* 251

Roger Mackenzie, 'The Future of Conveyancing' (2002) 47 *Journal of the Law Society of Scotland* Nov/21

Alan McMillan, 'Disability Discrimination Act' (2002) 58 *Greens Property Law Bulletin* 2

PAUL MOTION and GORDON BREWSTER, 'Electronic Signatures—Who Needs Them?' (2002) 47 *Journal of the Law Society of Scotland* Feb/44

RODERICK PAISLEY, 'Bower of Bliss?' (2002) 6 *Edinburgh Law Review* 101 (commenting on *Bowers v Kennedy* 2000 SC 555)

ROBERT RENNIE, 'Mineral Rights' (2002) 7 *Scottish Law & Practice Quarterly* 1

ROBERT RENNIE, 'Solicitors' Negligence: Rearguard Action' (2002) 7 *Scottish Law & Practice Quarterly* 87

ROSEANNE RUSSELL, '*Royal Bank of Scotland v Etridge (No 2)*' 2002 SLT (News) 55

ANDREW J M STEVEN, '*Sharp v Thomson*: a Reply' (2002) 70 *Scottish Law Gazette* 2

ANDREW J M STEVEN, 'Scottish Land Law in a State of Reform' 2002 *Journal of Business Law* 177

ANDREW J M STEVEN, 'Goodbye to the Landlord's Hypothec?' 2002 SLT (News) 177

ANDREW J M STEVEN, 'The Progress of Article 1, Protocol 1 in Scotland' (2002) 6 *Edinburgh Law Review* 396.

KEN SWINTON, 'Variable Mortgage Interest Rates' (2002) 70 *Scottish Law Gazette* 5

KEN SWINTON, 'Mortgages and Redemption Charges' (2002) 70 *Scottish Law Gazette* 32

KEN SWINTON, 'The House Buying Process in Scotland: Does it Need to be Fixed?' (2002) 70 *Scottish Law Gazette* 69

KEN SWINTON, 'Reform of the House Selling Process in England' (2002) 70 *Scottish Law Gazette* 103

KEN SWINTON, 'CML Handbook second edition' (2002) 70 *Scottish Law Gazette* 173

KEN SWINTON, 'The Regulation of Mortgage Advice' (2002) 70 *Scottish Law Gazette* 180

KEN SWINTON, 'Family Funded Purchases' (2002) 47 *Journal of the Law Society of Scotland* July/48

KEN SWINTON, 'Effective Continuing Powers of Attorney' 2002 SLT (News) 215

L P W VAN VLIET, 'Accession of Movables to Land' (2002) 6 *Edinburgh Law Review* 67 and 199

SCOTT WORTLEY, 'Double Sales and the Offside Trap: Some Thoughts on the Rule Penalising Private Knowledge of a Prior Right' 2002 *Juridical Review* 291

SCOTT WORTLEY and DOT REID, 'Mind the Gap: Problems in the Transfer of Ownership' (2002) 7 *Scottish Law & Practice Quarterly* 211

PART IV

COMMENTARY

MISSIVES OF SALE

Dates of entry and delay in settlement

Take the following, commonplace, example. Missives provide that

> Entry and actual occupation shall be given on 1 April 2003 or on such other date as may be mutually agreed between the parties.

In the event, settlement is delayed due to default by one of the parties. Eventually the transaction settles on 30 April, more than four weeks late. What is the date of entry? Is it 1 April or 30 April?

This very issue arose in *Spence v W & R Murray (Alford) Ltd*.[1] The sellers were unable to produce a title to the satisfaction of the buyers, with the result that matters dragged on, inconclusively, for several years. Eventually the buyers decided to take the plunge and settle the transaction. Now it was the sellers' turn to refuse. Clause 18 of the offer provided that

> This offer and the missives following hereon will form a continuing and enforceable contract notwithstanding the delivery of the disposition except in so far as fully implemented thereby. But the missives shall cease to be enforceable after a period of two years from the date of entry except in so far as they are founded on in any court proceedings.

More than two years had passed since the date stipulated in the missives for entry. Therefore, argued the sellers, the missives had expired.

The First Division agreed. According to Lord President Cullen[2]

> [T]he expression 'the date of entry' has a well recognised meaning as the date on which entry was to be given in accordance with the missives, subject to any other agreement between the parties to a different effect. The pursuers did not negotiate an alteration of the running of the two-year period provided in cl 18 when matters took longer to be resolved than anticipated.

Whatever the logical attractions of this position, the result in the particular case is startling. A clause inserted for the benefit of the purchaser[3] ends up by

1 2002 SLT 918.
2 2002 SLT 918 at 919L–920A.
3 Missives were concluded in 1993, before the enactment of the Contract (Scotland) Act 1997, s 2. Today supersession clauses are inserted for the benefit of the seller.

defeating his rights. And delay said to have been caused by fault of the sellers ends up by excusing them from further performance of their obligations.

It is tempting to view the decision in *Spence* as confined to its own, rather peculiar, facts. It is not. Much, of course, depends on the way that missives happen to be drafted. But many sets of missives, and many standard offers, are vulnerable to the argument which succeeded in *Spence*. And a number of different clauses are likely to be affected. The risk clause, for example, may tie the passing of risk to the 'date of entry'. If so, then, on the authority of *Spence*, risk passes on the date which is contractually stipulated, regardless of when settlement actually takes place. This means that the buyers are at risk even if the sellers remain in possession and were the cause of the delay. Similarly, any warranty given by the sellers as at the 'date of entry' will be devalued in the event that settlement is delayed.

It might be taken from these examples that the desired date will always be the date on which settlement *actually* takes place, rather than the date for which it was contracted. But in fact matters are not so simple. For example, the familiar clause providing for payment of interest on the price is often triggered by a failure to pay on the 'date of entry'. If 'date of entry' meant 'date of settlement', no interest would ever be due.

The truth is that, in cases of delay in settlement, there are at least two different dates to be borne in mind. One is the contractual date of entry. The other is the date on which settlement actually takes place. Missives often fail to discriminate between the two. The lesson of *Spence* is that more care is required.

As long ago as 1988 one of the authors drew attention to the difficulty and suggested as a possible solution a clause along the following lines:[1]

> Entry and actual occupation shall be given to the purchaser on 1 April 2003 or on such other date as may be mutually agreed between the parties ('date of entry'). In this offer and the missives to follow hereon 'date of settlement' means the date on which settlement is actually effected whether that is the date of entry or some other date.

It would then be a matter of going through the standard offer carefully, and deciding which dates should refer to entry and which to settlement.

Other approaches are possible. For example, in clauses directed at settlement the language of entry could be abandoned altogether and replaced with a reference to a particular event, such as delivery of the disposition, or the taking of possession. A potential advantage of this approach is to cover the possibility that entry, delivery of the disposition and payment all occur on different days, meaning that there is no single date of settlement.[2] Thus for instance, the passing of risk could be tied to the date on which the buyer takes possession, and the supersession of missives to the date of delivery of the disposition.

1 K G C Reid, 'Date of Entry or Date of Settlement?' (1988) 33 *Journal of the Law Society of Scotland* 431.

2 G L Gretton, 'Date of Entry or Date of Settlement?' (1989) 34 *Journal of the Law Society of Scotland* 175.

A difficulty faced by any approach is that the buyer is not the sole author of the contract, so that, even if the offer is scrupulous in distinguishing the different dates, the qualified acceptances (unless watched carefully) may fail to do so.

Supersession clauses: starting the clock

The accident rate in supersession clauses continues to be surprisingly high. *Spence v W & R Murray* has just been mentioned. There the clock for the two-year period started prematurely, with the result that the period had expired before the missives were implemented. But at least the clock started. *Lonergan v W & P Food Service Ltd*[1] was a case in which it failed to start at all. The clause read:

> The missives shall remain in full force and effect until fully implemented notwithstanding payment of the price and delivery of the disposition but that for a period of two years only except in so far as they are founded on in any court proceedings which have commenced within the said period . . .

But when was the two-year period to start? A conveyancer would say, without hesitation, that it started on the day when the price was paid and the disposition delivered; and, if pressed, the conveyancer would probably add that, in the unlikely event that payment and delivery occurred on different days, the period started on the later of those days. Lord Clarke, in the Outer House of the Court of Session, was less accommodating. In his view the clause did not disclose any starting point. Therefore it was void for uncertainty.[2] This decision further emphasises the importance of absolute clarity in relation to dates.

STANDARD SECURITIES

Calling up and sequestration

In *Clydesdale Bank plc v McCaw*[3] the defender granted a standard security to the pursuers in 1990. The defender was sequestrated in 1992. For a time the DSS paid the interest on the secured loan, but when that ended the bank sought to enforce the security. In 2000 the bank served a calling-up notice, and later the same year they raised the present action. What was concluded for is not quite clear, but seemingly there was the usual mix of craves seeking declarator of the creditor's rights as arising out of the notice. The sheriff granted summary decree. The defender, who was a party litigant, appealed to the sheriff principal, who also found against her. She appealed to the Inner House, which has now also found against her.

---

1 2002 SLT 908.

2 In Lord Clarke's words (at p 913E), 'I cannot accede to senior counsel for the defenders' submission that I should simply imply, as a starting date, the date of delivery of the disposition or the date of entry, having regard to what he described as the "background of case law" and the intention of the parties.'

3 2002 GWD 18-603.

When the pursuers raised their action it was taken for granted that the defender's trustee in sequestration had been discharged. But during the course of the action it emerged that this was not the case, and it also came to light that the calling-up notice, though served on the defender, had not been served on her trustee in sequestration, as is required by s 19(3) of the Conveyancing and Feudal Reform (Scotland) Act 1970. The pursuers produced evidence that the trustee had disclaimed any interest in the property, and also that the trustee had been given an opportunity to intervene in the action but had decided not to do so. On that basis it was held that the failure to serve the notice on the trustee was irrelevant for the purposes of the present action.

This decision is no doubt sound as far as it goes, but it raises some interesting issues. One concerns vesting, revesting and abandonment. It is sometimes mistakenly supposed that when a debtor is discharged, which normally happens after three years, any unrealised property revests. That is not so. Assets that have fallen under the sequestration remain subject to the sequestration notwithstanding the debtor's discharge—which is why, in the present case, the position of the trustee remained crucial, even many years after sequestration. The debtor's discharge does not bring about revesting. But this vital doctrine has two qualifications.

The first qualification is the doctrine of abandonment, ie the doctrine that a trustee in sequestration can choose to abandon an asset. The effect of abandonment is that the asset in question ceases to be subject to the sequestration and revests in the debtor. The doctrine, though important in practice, is one on which there is little authority. In the present case it seems that the court took the view that the trustee had abandoned the property, though since that technical term is not used it is hard to be sure. If the trustee had abandoned the property, there can be no doubt that s 19(3) of the 1970 Act would be implicitly disapplied.

The second qualification is that a trustee who wishes to keep rights to heritable property alive for more than three years after the opening of the sequestration must either complete title or register a notice under s 14(4) of the Bankruptcy (Scotland) Act 1985. Failure to do either of these—and such failures are remarkably common in practice—may result in the loss of the property, because of the little-known provisions of s 44(4) of the Conveyancing (Scotland) Act 1924, as amended.

What if there had been no evidence before the court to enable it to conclude that the trustee had abandoned the property? Would the defence based on s 19(3) have been successful? The opinion of the court does not answer that question. It is certainly a difficult one. There is a strong case for saying that the right to plead non-service is a right that belongs only to the person on whom service was not made, so that the debtor cannot plead that service was not made on someone else. If that analysis is correct, it would not necessarily help the creditor, for a purchaser (and/or the Keeper) could, in such circumstances, object to the title, on the basis that a decree granted against the debtor, after the opening of the sequestration, would not normally be *res judicata* against the trustee. But there is another way of looking at matters, namely that the calling-up procedure is a unitary procedure, that a failure in one part is a failure in the whole, and that there cannot therefore be a 'limping' calling-up, ie a calling-up which is valid against some parties but not against others. We offer no definite opinion as to which of these two possible approaches is correct, but would merely say that we incline towards the second.

It is remarkable how often heritable property falls under a sequestration and yet the trustee does not seek to realise it. Negative equity is a common reason, and was the reason in the *McCaw* case. But—and here we leave the *McCaw* case itself behind and make general observations—what was negative equity at the time of the sequestration can, because of changing property values, become positive equity after a few years, and in this context the trustee can afford to wait because the debtor's discharge does not affect the trustee's rights.

Moreover, occasionally negative equity is an illusion anyway. The fact that the property is worth £250,000 and the amount owed to the bank is £450,000 does not necessarily mean that there is negative equity of £200,000. It is possible that, when a full study is made, it will emerge that not all the debt was secured debt. Not all standard securities are vanilla-flavour all-sums standard securities, securing all debts due or to become due. And even where the standard security is in such terms, it may be that subsequent arrangements have an impact. One example would be where, some years after the granting of the standard security, the bank makes a further loan which is expressly agreed to be secured *solely* upon a *different* property. The fact that the standard security over the *first* property was for all sums is arguably now irrelevant, for any agreement which bears to regulate future dealings can always be varied by a *later* agreement between the same parties. The counter-argument would be that variations of standard securities have to be registered, as a result of s 16 of the Conveyancing and Feudal Reform (Scotland) Act 1970. The meaning and effect of s 16 are obscure, but it is worth noticing that in comparable cases the courts have been reluctant to deny effect to unregistered agreements: see *Scottish & Newcastle plc v Ascot Inns Ltd* and *Bank of Ireland v Bass Brewers Ltd.*[1]

Cautionary wives

The saga of the cautionary wives[2] has kept the courts busy for several years.[3] One partner to the marriage, generally the wife, is asked to guarantee a loan to the other partner, or his company, or to grant a standard security for it over the family home. The loan is not repaid and the bank wishes to enforce. The wife claims that she signed as a result of undue influence or misrepresentation on the part of her husband. Is that plea a relevant defence as against the bank? The answer, until 1997, was no, unless the bank had some positive reason for supposing that the wife's consent might have been unfairly obtained. That traditional position was upheld by the Inner House in the combined cases of

1 *Scottish & Newcastle plc v Ascot Inns Ltd* 1994 SLT 1140; *Bank of Ireland v Bass Brewers Ltd* 2000 GWD 28-1077. See *Conveyancing 2000* pp 81–83.
2 The gendered language is deliberate. The gender-neutrality of this area of law is only nominal.
3 See *Conveyancing 1999* pp 54–56; *Conveyancing 2000* pp 86–91; *Conveyancing 2001* pp 92–96.

Mumford v Bank of Scotland and *Smith v Bank of Scotland* in 1996.[1] Mrs Smith appealed to the House of Lords, naturally enough, for there was hope that the House of Lords would apply English law, which is more or less what happened when the case was heard in 1997: *Smith v Bank of Scotland*.[2]

At that time, the leading English case was the decision of the House of Lords in *Barclays Bank v O'Brien*.[3] Since 1997 there have been many more English decisions (as well as the large crop of Scottish ones), but one is of particular importance, being the first decision of the House of Lords on an English case since *O'Brien* itself, namely *Royal Bank of Scotland plc v Etridge (No 2)*.[4] The new Scottish case of *Clydesdale Bank plc v Black* was working its way through the lower courts when *Etridge* was decided, and has now gone to the Inner House as a result.[5] The key issue was whether *Etridge* should be regarded as authoritative in Scots law; and the answer is no.

The facts were that on 8 November 1996 Mrs Black signed a guarantee of her husband's liabilities to the bank, limited to £50,000 plus interest. The document was as prescribed under the Consumer Credit Act 1974, and thus contained lots of warnings in big black letters, for instance:

> Under this guarantee and indemnity YOU MAY HAVE TO PAY INSTEAD of the debtor and fulfil any other obligations under the guarantee and indemnity.[6]

At about this time Mrs Black instructed her own firm of solicitors to negotiate a standard security over the family home (which was in her sole name) to the bank, and after a few days the deed was sent to her for signing. It was sent directly by the bank's solicitors, with a covering letter:

> You should contact your solicitors to discuss the legal implications of signing this document prior to doing so. We wish to make it clear that we are acting solely on the bank's behalf in this matter and can give you no advice as to whether indeed you should sign this document. We understand that your solicitors wish you to return the document to them as soon as it is signed.

Mrs Black duly signed, her husband signed as consenter, and the deed was registered. The inevitable then ensued, and the bank sought to enforce the guarantee and standard security. Mrs Black's defence was that she had not understood what she was signing, and that her two signatures had been procured by the undue influence of her husband. It was held, affirming the decision of the sheriff principal, that no relevant defences had been put forward, and decree *de plano* was granted in favour of the pursuers.

---

1 1996 SLT 392.
2 1997 SC (HL) 111, 1997 SLT 1061.
3 [1994] 1 AC 180.
4 [2001] 4 All ER 449. For a Scottish view of this case, see an article by Roseanne Russell published at 2002 SLT (News) 55. And see *Conveyancing 2001* pp 94–96.
5 2002 SLT 764, 2002 SCLR 857. For discussion see Mark Higgins at 2002 SLT (News) 173.
6 It added: 'But you cannot be made to pay more than he could have been made to pay *unless he is under 18*'. (Our italics.) History does not record what Mrs Black made of this strange sentence. Perhaps she thought that it meant that teenage husbands cost more.

In both *O'Brien* and *Etridge* the House of Lords laid down detailed rules as to what must be done to shield the bank from defences based on undue influence or misrepresentation.[1] The core issue in *Black* was whether these detailed rules apply also in Scots law. Decisions of the House of Lords in English cases are not strictly binding in Scotland unless they construe legislation that is common to both countries. Nevertheless, such decisions tend to be strongly persuasive. In *Mumford* the Inner House could decline to follow the English decisions since the law of Scotland was at that time clearly quite different from the English law. But in *Smith* the House of Lords held that Scots law must follow English law, and so it was inevitable, from that moment on, that English decisions in this area would assume a significance which they had not had previously. What nobody could know was how significant.

The possibility that Scotland might be allowed a certain degree of autonomy was clear from the start. For in *Smith* Lord Clyde, who gave the leading opinion,[2] said that whilst Scots law should adopt the English rule as to its substance, it should not adopt it as to its form, or, in other words, as to its theoretical foundation. The rule for Scots law, he said, should be based on the idea of good faith. A creditor who takes caution owes a duty of good faith to the cautioner. Given that the House of Lords was going to decide as it did, this choice of good faith as the theoretical basis was a good one. There is a touch of heather-and-tartan about it, for good faith is a doctrine which does have a certain role in the Scottish law of obligations, albeit not so strong a role as in many Continental jurisdictions.[3] The fact that the Scottish version of *O'Brien* had a different theoretical basis allowed for the possibility that the Scottish doctrine would not necessarily follow the English rules in all their twists and turns. In *Black* the Court of Session had to decide whether that possibility would be allowed to develop into actuality, or whether Scots law would simply follow English law. As Lord Coulsfield put it:[4]

> The more difficult question is whether the extension of the *O'Brien* decision to Scotland requires the Scottish courts to apply the same underlying test in determining whether the creditor has acted in good faith as the English courts apparently require to do in determining whether the creditor is or is not affected by constructive notice.

1 As Lord Sutherland said in *Black* (2002 SLT 764 at 775J), 'the decision in that case [*Etridge*] was to add yet further steps to be taken for the future by lenders in England to avoid being held to have constructive notice of the risk of undue influence being exerted against the guarantor.'

2 Lord Jauncey also spoke briefly. Like Lord Clyde, he considered that the decision of the Inner House was right, but should nevertheless be reversed. 'Applying the principles of Scots law alone I would therefore have been disposed to dismiss this appeal. Nevertheless I am conscious that your Lordships do not share my difficulties and I appreciate the practical advantages of applying the same law to identical transactions in both jurisdictions. In these circumstances I do not feel able to dissent from your Lordships' view that the appeal should be allowed.'

3 The question of the role of good faith in Scots law has been a matter of controversy of course, and to some extent remains so. See generally A D M Forte (ed), *Good Faith in Contract and Property* (1999).

4 2002 SLT 764 at 771F.

The three judges involved, Lords Coulsfield, Marnoch and Sutherland, gave separate opinions, and there is room for debate as to what extent these opinions did or did not coincide. But it seems that all three were agreed that the detailed rules laid down in *Etridge* are not part of Scots law. One suspects that they peered over the precipice and recoiled. The English law in this area is spectacularly complex, incomprehensible to outsiders and in the last analysis perhaps internally incoherent.

All three judges accepted that the test for Scotland is the broad test set forth by Lord Clyde in *Smith*:[1]

> All that is required of him [ie the creditor] is that he should take reasonable steps to secure that in relation to the proposed contract he acts throughout in good faith. So far as the substance of those steps is concerned it seems to me that it would be sufficient for the creditor to warn the potential cautioner of the consequences of entering into the proposed cautionary obligation and to advise him or her to take independent advice.

Lord Marnoch was clear that the bank had satisfied that test. Lords Coulsfield and Sutherland were less clear on that point, for both took the view that, since the events in question had taken place in 1996, they were subject to the less demanding pre-*Smith* law. To explain this, a few more words about *Smith* are necessary. The traditional view of the role of the courts is that they are to declare the law, to interpret it, and to apply it to concrete cases, but they are not to alter rules which are clearly established. Changing the law is something that should be left to legislation. Moreover, experience shows that judicial legislation is often bad legislation. Law reform is difficult, and litigation, where the focus is on a single case and not the system in the round, and where a process of public consultation is impossible, is, it may be argued, an obviously unsuitable way for law reform to take place. Most judicial legislation, of course, is marginal and disguised. *Smith* was large-scale and overt, the House of Lords agreeing that the Court of Session had decided according to the law of Scotland but that the law of Scotland would be altered.

One of the difficulties with judicial legislation is that, unlike ordinary legislation, it is retroactive. What was lawful at the time is retrospectively deemed to have been unlawful. That is unfair. The logical treatment of judicial legislation is to treat it literally as legislation, so that it applies only for the future.[2] That seems to have been the approach of Lords Coulsfield and Sutherland. We are aware of only one other case in Scottish legal history where a House of Lords' decision was treated by the Court of Session as naked legislation and for that reason as inapplicable to past facts: that was *Home v Pringle* in 1841.[3]

Where does *Black* leave matters? Negatively, it decides that *Etridge* is not law in Scotland. It *may* also decide, again negatively, that *Smith* does not apply to

---

1 1997 SC (HL) 111 at 122.

2 Logical, but logic is a dangerous thing, for it may lead to rational conclusions. Thus if *Smith* was judicial legislation, Mrs Smith should have *lost*, for the facts in Smith were, from the nature of time itself, pre-*Smith* facts.

3 (1841) 2 Rob 384. See *Miller's Trs v Miller* (1848) 10 D 765.

pre-1997 transactions. It does not give much positive guidance to the solicitor advising the cautionary wife, other than that what the law requires seems to be less stringent than under English law. The non-applicability of *Etridge* is good news for solicitors. But it remains necessary to show the utmost circumspection when dealing with cautionary wives.

REAL BURDENS

Rights of pre-emption

Back in 1988 rights of pre-emption were challenged as being clauses *de non aliendo sine consensu superiorum* and hence as unlawful under s 10 of the Tenures Abolition Act 1746.[1] Less exotically but no more promisingly, a new case, *Macdonald-Haig v Gerlings*,[2] follows current fashion by challenging pre-emptions under the European Convention on Human Rights. The pre-emption in question was for a fixed sum (augmented according to a formula to take some account of improvements) rather than, as usually, for the price the market was willing to pay. As a result the sum due was less than half the market value of the property. The exercise of such a pre-emption, it was argued by the current owner, would be a deprivation of a possession under article 1 of the First Protocol to the ECHR without adequate compensation. Hence it could not lawfully be enforced by the courts on the, now familiar, basis that, by s 6(1) of the Human Rights Act 1998, a public authority (including a court) cannot act in a manner incompatible with a Convention right. This argument has a curious pre-echo in the *obiter dictum*, from a more innocent age, that a right of redemption will not be enforced as a real burden if the price is merely 'elusory'.[3]

The sheriff was unimpressed. In his view

> [T]he purpose of Article 1 is to protect individuals against a state seeking to deprive them of their possessions . . . Such deprivation could take a number of forms such as nationalisation or forced removal for some other purpose in terms of a statute pronounced by the relevant state. I am not persuaded that the terms of the Article can properly be applied to a situation such as the present where, in effect, the Defender seeks to avoid the consequences of a contract, the terms of which were known to him before he possessed the property, freely entered into between two private individuals, albeit two individuals other than the Defender himself.

Indeed, far from a pre-emption being contrary to the ECHR, a failure on the part of the court to enforce such a pre-emption would itself be a breach of the Convention. This idea—that a pre-emption is itself a 'possession' protected by the ECHR—may possibly lie behind the amendment, discussed below, made

1 *Matheson v Tinney* 1989 SLT 535. The challenge failed.
2 Inverness Sheriff Court, 3 December 2001 (unreported).
3 *McElroy v Duke of Argyll* (1902) 4 F 885 at 889 per Lord Kyllachy. This *dictum* does not seem to have been cited in *Macdonald-Haig*. Its basis, presumably, was public policy.

by the Title Conditions (Scotland) Bill to the Abolition of Feudal Tenure etc (Scotland) Act 2000 in relation to feudal pre-emptions.

In the event, another issue in *Macdonald-Haig* turned out to be more important. The pre-emption was contained in a disposition granted in 1980 by the pursuer to a Mrs Terpstra and a Mr Maas. It began:

> there is reserved to me *and my executors* a right of pre-emption over the said subjects exercisable on the sale of the subjects hereby disponed or on the death of the said Mrs … Terpstra, whichever is the earlier.

Since only sales were struck at, the disponees were free to make a gift, which in 1997 they duly did, disponing the house to Mrs Terpstra and to her son, the defender in the current action, and to the survivor. When Mrs Terpstra died on 30 November 1999, this activated both the survivorship clause and the pre-emption. Accordingly, the pursuer claimed the property from the defender.

An oddity in the wording of the pre-emption is the reference to executors. Where, as here, a pre-emption is created in a disposition (as opposed to a feu disposition), it binds successors if and only if the enforcement right is tied to ownership of some other property in the neighbourhood. There must, in the language of the Title Conditions Bill, be a 'benefited property' as well as a 'burdened property'. In this respect a pre-emption is in the same position as any other real burden. Naturally a well-drafted clause will nominate the benefited property expressly. Where, however, this is not done, it is generally implied that the benefited property is such other property in the neighbourhood as is retained by the granter.[1] The law, in other words, steps in and makes up for the conveyancer's omission.

The clause in *Macdonald-Haig* made no mention of a benefited property, and no averments were made to the effect that one could be implied, the case being argued on the basis that, with the 1980 disposition, the pursuer had disposed of all her property in that particular area. From this point on the outcome was inevitable.[2] In the absence of a benefited property there could be no real burden; and in the absence of a real burden the pre-emption could not bind a singular successor such as the defender. At most it was enforceable contractually, by the original parties to the disposition. But the original disponees no longer owned the house. The action, accordingly, was dismissed.

The decision is a useful reminder that pre-emptions in dispositions bind successors only where there is neighbouring land to act as a benefited property. A person cannot both sell all of his or her land and at the same time impose a pre-emption which will bind successors. The position for feu dispositions is different, for the pre-emption attaches to the reserved superiority, and ownership of neighbouring land is relevant, if at all, only in relation to interest to enforce.[3]

---

1 *J A Mactaggart & Co v Harrower* (1906) 8 F 1101.

2 The argument in the case proceeded on the detailed examination of the law of pre-emptions contained in part 10 of the Scottish Law Commission's *Report on Real Burdens* (Scot Law Com no 181, 2000, available on www.scotlawcom.gov.uk).

3 And the position here is uncertain and controversial. See K G C Reid, *The Law of Property in Scotland* (1996) para 408.

The position will change fundamentally on 28 November 2004, with feudal abolition. In the first place, feu dispositions will, obviously, cease to be available. But, secondly, even in ordinary dispositions the rule that a benefited property can be implied will no longer operate. Instead, if a disposition granted after feudal abolition seeks to impose a real burden, it must nominate a benefited property, and indeed the real burden must be registered against the title of that property, as well as being registered against the title of the burdened property. Otherwise there will be no real burden, and no question of a pre-emption binding successors.[1]

Finally, mention may be made of an amendment to the Abolition of Feudal Tenure etc (Scotland) Act 2000 by the Title Conditions (Scotland) Bill, currently before the Scottish Parliament. Pre-emptions, like other feudal burdens, may be saved by superiors by registration of a notice to that effect before 28 November 2004.[2] But, as the 2000 Act currently stands, the notice must nominate land as a replacement benefited property; and, having regard to the praedial rule, that land must be reasonably nearby.[3] The idea is that the pre-emption right should pass from the superiority to the neighbouring land. If, therefore, a superior does not own neighbouring land, the pre-emption cannot be preserved. The result is that certain pre-emptions which, on one view of the law at least, are currently enforceable are not capable of being rescued from feudal abolition. The amendment in the Title Conditions Bill is designed to remedy this omission.[4] The device of preservation by reference to a neighbouring property remains. But superiors are given the alternative of saving pre-emptions in a personal capacity, without reference to any property. The pre-emption thus saved is then a 'personal pre-emption burden', a real burden without a benefited property. This is a transitional provision only, and there is no question of personal pre-emptions being created in the future.[5] Further, such feudal pre-emptions as are saved are likely to have a short life because of the rule, re-enacted in s 75 of the Title Conditions Bill, that a pre-emption is extinguished on the first occasion on which the property is offered back.

Service charges and other indefinite payments

Since service charges vary from year to year, an obligation to pay such a charge is necessarily expressed quite generally, with no actual amount stipulated; and in practice such charges are accepted as valid and are paid without question. Yet it has quite often been doubted whether, in strict law, they are enforceable.[6]

---

1 Title Conditions (Scotland) Bill, ss 3(5), 4 and 45.
2 Abolition of Feudal Tenure etc (Scotland) Act 2000, s 18. By s 18(7)(b)(ii) the 100-metres rule does not apply in respect of rights of pre-emption.
3 The praedial rule is preserved by the Title Conditions (Scotland) Bill, s 3(3). There is also a question as to interest to enforce, as to which see s 8(3).
4 Title Conditions (Scotland) Bill, s 102(2), adding a new s 18A to the 2000 Act.
5 This is because, despite the mention of personal pre-emption burdens in s 1(3) of the Title Conditions Bill, no provision is made for the creation of such burdens in the future.
6 K G C Reid, *The Law of Property in Scotland* (1996) para 418(4); R Rennie, 'The Reality of Real Burdens' 1998 SLT (News) 149 at 151–152.

The difficulty indeed goes right back to the foundational case in the law of real burdens, the decision in *Tailors of Aberdeen v Coutts*, where the House of Lords declined to enforce an obligation to defray a cost because, among other reasons, 'it is an obligation to pay . . . an unascertained sum of money, which it is on all hands agreed cannot be imposed'.[1] A real burden for payment of money must, on this view, stipulate the amount that is due. And the difficulty is not confined to service charges but would apply also to standard maintenance obligations in the titles of tenements and other properties. Indeed, in respect of maintenance obligations, this approach would seek to draw a distinction between (1) a direct obligation to maintain property (which is enforceable) and (2) an indirect obligation to defray the cost of maintaining property (which, on this approach, is not).[2] Over the years the question of what *Tailors of Aberdeen* really meant on this point has been the subject of dispute, and there have been a number of later authorities, none very satisfactory. But, curiously, the matter has never been properly tested in litigation.

A new decision, *Sheltered Housing Management Ltd v Cairns*,[3] contains some helpful, albeit *obiter*, remarks on this topic. In the view of Lord Nimmo Smith:[4]

> Consideration of these authorities does not persuade me that provision for payment of a service charge of unspecified amount would be unenforceable as a real burden. In *Tailors of Aberdeen v Coutts* Lord Brougham, having held that an obligation to pay an unascertained sum of money cannot be imposed, went on to say that the obligation to pay the expense or any proportion of the expense of repairing, immediately connected with the subject granted, 'would clearly stand in a different predicament'. The provision of services by a management company in a sheltered housing complex appears to me to be immediately connected with the properties within that complex, and the payment of a service charge, albeit of an amount only ascertainable by reference to the concept of reasonableness, as the counterpart to provision of those services appears to me also to stand in the 'different predicament' contemplated by Lord Brougham.

Any doubt still remaining will be removed on 28 November 2004 when the Title Conditions (Scotland) Bill comes into force. By s 5(1) of that Bill:[5]

> It shall not be an objection to the validity of a real burden (whenever created) that—
>
> (a) an amount payable in respect of an obligation to defray some cost is not specified in the constitutive deed; . . .

The effect of the words '(whenever created)' is that the provision is retrospective.

---

1 (1840) 1 Rob 296 at 340 per Lord Brougham.

2 However, for a case decided in 2002 where an obligation to defray the cost of maintenance *was* enforced, see *Quantum Claims Compensation Specialists Ltd v Findlay* 2002 GWD 22-733.

3 2002 Hous LR 126. The case is mainly about judicial rectification, and is discussed further in that context at p 97.

4 2002 Hous LR 126 at para 22.

5 See further Scottish Law Commission, *Report on Real Burdens* (Scot Law Com no 181, 2000) paras 3.21–3.24.

A common feature of service charges in sheltered housing complexes is that the amount due can be increased, in an upwards direction, by the superiors/managers at their sole discretion, sometimes indeed without consultation or explanation.[1] Another helpful aspect of Lord Nimmo Smith's judgment is the suggestion of an implied condition that any such increase would have to be reasonable.

Unregistered rules

Another aspect of *Sheltered Housing Management Ltd v Cairns*[2] is worthy of brief comment. The deed of conditions[3] provided that

> A Management Scheme comprising regulations shall be drawn up by the Superiors and these shall be enforceable against the feuars. These Management Regulations shall contain rules governing the management and administration of the complex and the payment of Charges by the feuars for such management and administration. The Management Scheme shall contain, but shall not be limited to, the following rules . . . [a list of five rules followed]

If the burdens in the deed of conditions are thought of as primary legislation, these projected rules are secondary legislation, a kind of statutory instrument to be drawn up by the superiors in the exercise of the powers conferred by the deed of conditions. It is hardly conceivable that rules made in this way could be enforceable in a question with successors of the original feuars.[4] The law here is strict, and for sound reasons. The terms of real burdens must be set out in full in the deed of conditions or other constitutive deed. This is sometimes called the 'four corners of the deed rule'. And the deed must be registered, so that the obligations are properly publicised, and hence discoverable by future purchasers and other third parties.[5] Even minor deviations from this rule have been punished with invalidity,[6] for the law does not allow a purchaser to be ambushed by conditions which do not appear on the Register.

The Title Conditions Bill does not change the position but rather reinforces it by providing that the registered deed must 'set out' the terms of any real burden.[7] One exception only is allowed. In cases where the (optional) Development Management Scheme is used, the owners' association under that Scheme is empowered to make regulations as to the use of recreational facilities (only). Such regulations are not registered although a copy must be sent to every owner. Regulations on other matters are not permitted.[8]

---

1 For an explanation of two different models, see paras 4–6 of Lord Nimmo Smith's opinion.
2 2002 Hous LR 126.
3 As, ultimately, rectified in consequence of the action.
4 The matter, however, does not appear to have been raised. The five rules actually listed in the deed might, however, be enforceable as real burdens in their own terms.
5 What is sometimes called the 'publicity principle' is one of the major themes underlying property law.
6 Most notably *Aberdeen Varieties Ltd v James F Donald (Aberdeen Cinemas Ltd)* 1939 SC 788.
7 Title Conditions (Scotland) Bill, s 4(2)(a).
8 Scottish Law Commission, *Report on Real Burdens* (Scot Law Com no 181, 2000) para 8.61.

SOLICITORS

Indemnity insurance and intentional wrongs

In 1990 Cheltenham & Gloucester Building Society made a loan to Mr and Mrs Gallagher, to be secured over a property in Bishopbriggs. A term of the offer of loan was that:

> The Society requires this mortgage [*sic*] to be registered as a first charge [*sic*]. All other charges must be either repaid or postponed.

The Cheltenham & Gloucester instructed the clients' solicitor (a sole practitioner) to act for them. At the time there were two standard securities over the property, the first to the Bank of Scotland and the second to the Clydesdale Bank. The solicitor encashed the loan cheque, paid off the Clydesdale Bank loan, and paid the balance to his clients. The new standard security was recorded, but was, of course, a second-ranking security. By way of background, it appears that the solicitor had close relations with the clients, and it seems that he himself had been a cautioner for the Clydesdale Bank loan.

The clients became insolvent and the Bank of Scotland enforced its security by sale. The proceeds of sale did not even meet the debt due to the Bank of Scotland, so there was nothing for the Cheltenham & Gloucester. The latter sued the borrowers, but were unable to recover any part of the loan. They then sued the solicitor for damages, for having failed to obtain a first-ranking standard security. They obtained decree. But the damages could not be recovered, because he was sequestrated.

The solicitor was, of course, insured under the Master Policy. Under the Third Parties (Rights against Insurers) Act 1930, where a person with indemnity insurance becomes bankrupt, the right against the insurer vests directly in the injured third party. Hence Cheltenham & Gloucester had title to claim direct from Sun Alliance. But the latter declined to pay, and litigation ensued. The earlier stages of this litigation were mentioned in previous volumes.[1] The case has now finally gone to proof, and the action has failed.[2]

The Master Policy provided:

> The insurers will indemnify the insured:
>
> 1. Against liability at law for damages and claimant's costs and expenses in respect of claims or alleged claims made against the Insured and notified to the Brokers during the Period of Insurance specified in the Schedule by reason of any negligent act, neglect, error or omission on the part of
>   (a) the Insured or the predecessors of the Practice;
>   (b) any agent or correspondent of the insured or of the predecessors of the Practice;

1 *Cheltenham & Gloucester plc v Sun Alliance and London Insurance plc* 2001 SLT 347 (discussed in *Conveyancing 2000* pp 116–117) *rev* 2001 SLT 1151 (discussed in *Conveyancing 2001* pp 30–32).

2 *Cheltenham & Gloucester plc v Sun Alliance and London Insurance plc (No 2)* 2002 GWD 18-605.

occurring or committed or alleged to have occurred or to have been committed in good faith in connection with the Practice.

5. If any claim be in any respect fraudulent or if any fraudulent means or devices be used by the Insured or anyone acting on the Insured's behalf to obtain benefit under this Certificate all benefit hereunder in respect of the individual or individuals committing or condoning the fraud shall be forfeited.

The defenders had three arguments to support their denial of liability. The first was that the solicitor had not acted negligently but deliberately. The second was that, whether or not he had acted deliberately, he had not acted in good faith. The third was forgery.

When everything went wrong, the solicitor argued that there had been an agreement with the Bank of Scotland that the latter would enter a ranking agreement which would give a first ranking to the Cheltenham & Gloucester. The bank had then failed to do this. He had meant to chase them, but he had left the matter to his assistant, who had let matters slip. In other words, the solicitor's position was that the fault had not really been his, except in a technical sense, and that the real fault was to be shared by the Bank of Scotland, which had not honoured its word, and his assistant, who had failed to chase the bank. If this was true, the loss was caused by mere negligence and the insurers would pick up the bill.

When the claim was intimated to them, the insurers instructed Neil Douglas (now Sheriff Douglas) of Messrs Brechin Robb. When Mr Douglas examined the file, he noticed something odd. There was a file note recording a telephone conversation between the solicitor and the Bank of Scotland.

Note for the file—Gallagher re-mortgage. 31 August 1990.

Phoning David Young, Bank of Scotland (Glasgow Chief Office) discussing the need for ranking agreement. Going over forms of letter of 28 August. Pointing out that bank presently ranks Second to Clydesdale Bank and that the re-mortgage simply substitutes new lender for the Clydesdale Bank.[1] Bank in no worse position. Noting should be no problem and that he will contact McClure Naismith regarding this.

Engaged: 10 minutes.

This file note supported the solicitor's story. What struck Mr Douglas, an experienced lawyer, as odd was that it was the *only* file note in the whole file. He became a little suspicious. He contacted David Young and discovered that on 31 August 1990 Mr Young was enjoying his summer vacation—in Italy. Mr Young even had the flight ticket stubs to prove the dates. Despite this the solicitor kept to his story. It was only when the proof came—and a dramatic moment in court it must have been—that the solicitor admitted that he had been lying, and admitted that he had forged the note and inserted it into the file two years later. It should perhaps be added that the assistant also gave evidence to the effect that she had never had anything to do with these clients. She was, in the words

1 In fact the Bank of Scotland were first-ranked and the Clydesdale second-ranked.

of the judge (Lord Clarke), 'a wholly credible and reliable' witness, unlike the solicitor, who was 'a very unsatisfactory witness'.

The defenders were successful in all three of their arguments—even though they needed to succeed in only one to win. As to the first (actions deliberate not negligent), Lord Clarke found that the solicitor:

> acted deliberately, knowingly and intentionally, with clear knowledge of the true position, in breach of his instructions from the pursuers. I am also satisfied that [he] had no basis for supposing that, in due course, the Bank of Scotland would, apparently for no consideration, be prepared to agree to give up their position as first-ranking security holders. The general principle of indemnity insurance law is that the insured cannot recover indemnity for deliberately bringing about the act insured against.

As to the second line of defence (bad faith), Lord Clarke found that the solicitor had not acted in good faith. As to the third (forgery), he found that one of the reasons why the solicitor had forged the file note was to make possible an insurance claim, thus activating the provisions of the General Condition 5 quoted above.

The significance of the case is obvious. The solicitor in question was a sole practitioner, and so had no partners to suffer from his actions. In a partnership a successful repudiation of liability on the part of the insurers might have drastic consequences for the partners of the culpable partner, as well as for that partner her/himself. At the same time, the decision should not cause panic. This was an extreme case. Everyone makes mistakes from time to time. Sometimes the mistakes, happily, have no adverse consequences—*injuria sine damno*. Sometimes they do. But honest negligence is precisely what liability insurance is all about. The honestly negligent solicitor has nothing to fear. Nor do his or her partners.

File notes and septic tanks

The previous case involved a file note but no conversation. The next case, *Wylie v Jeffrey Aitken*,[1] involves a conversation but no file note. A company entered into missives to buy a public house, namely the Bridge Inn, Linlithgow Bridge. The missives provided:

> The premises are at present served by a septic tank and the seller will, at his sole expense prior to the said date of entry, have the premises connected into the public sewage system and evidence of this would require to be exhibited to us prior to the said date of entry along with confirmation from the local sewerage authority that they were satisfied with the connection.

This was met by the following qualification, which itself was accepted without modification by the buyers:

> With regard to your condition 28, while our clients have already made contact with the Local Authority with regard to the installation of a connection to the public sewage system, it may be some time before this can be completed. Our clients will accordingly

1 2002 GWD 40-1360.

> identify the cost of the proposed connection and in the event of the work not having been completed prior to the said date of entry, a sum equivalent to the cost of carrying out such works will be held back from the purchase price by you to be placed on a joint interest-bearing deposit until the works have actually been completed. While our clients will be responsible for the negotiation and placing of the contract for the connection works, the actual works themselves will be instructed by your client who will be in day-to-day control of the premises. On completion of the works, the moneys held on deposit will be released to meet the account. In the event of the moneys on account not being sufficient to meet the relevant bills, our clients will remain responsible for any shortfall. Similarly if any money is left over after payment of the account, that over-provision will be repaid to our clients.

What happened now is not wholly clear: the following is a reconstruction which may not be perfectly accurate. The transaction settled without the work having been done. A retention of £10,400 was made. The purchasers installed a new system, which was a new septic tank and not a public connection. This proved inadequate. In the words of the Temporary Judge (Coutts QC), 'the inadequate sewage disposal caused smell and custom was lost. By 1997 the pursuer said that really the only trade came from outside the area, since locals were not coming'.[1] To what extent, if any, the sellers made a financial contribution is unclear, as is the fate of the £10,400 retention. The managing director of the purchasers, as assignee, sued his solicitors for damages for professional negligence in the sum of £125,000. The claim was based on an averment that a partner of the firm had advised the purchasers to proceed as they did. Everything turned on a telephone conversation. The solicitor concerned had made no file note.[2] After proof it was held that on balance of probabilities the solicitor had not advised the purchasers to act as they did, and decree of absolvitor was accordingly pronounced.

The case is of considerable practical interest. The pursuer argued that where client and solicitor differ in their recollection of a conversation, and the solicitor has nothing on file (whether by a file note or by an outgoing letter), then the presumption must be that the client's recollection is to be preferred. The pursuer referred to *Jackson & Powell on Professional Negligence*[3] para 10-174 which cites a Canadian case, *Morton v Harper Gray & Easton*,[4] apparently supporting the presumption in favour of the client's version. The text of *Jackson & Powell* is worth quoting:

> The solicitor is unlikely to recall after a period of several years what advice he gave to the client on a routine matter. The best that he can do is to describe his usual advice in the particular circumstances or to speculate as to what he 'must' have said, which is unlikely to carry as much weight as the recollection of the plaintiff. There is no proper substitute for a proper attendance note . . .

---

1 Paragraph 18 of the opinion.
2 '[He] kept few, if any, file notes at all at that time dealing with meetings and telephone conversations', observed the judge at para 10.
3 R M Jackson (ed), *Jackson & Powell on Professional Negligence* (5th edn, 2001).
4 (1995) 8 BCLR (2d) 53 (Supreme Court of British Columbia).

Temporary Judge Coutts was not prepared to follow *Morton*:[1]

> The absence of file notes do [*sic*] not raise any presumption. It is for the pursuer to prove his case and if it be thought that on any matter of fact opposing parties were on equal ground, whether or not one or other party made a note at the time, does not in my view form a proper basis for deciding a case.

He held, after proof, that the evidence of the solicitor was to be preferred. There were various reasons for coming to that conclusion, one of them being that 'it is inherently improbable that a conveyancer would give advice about the suitability or otherwise of a sewage system'.[2]

This decision will be welcomed by conveyancers. However, despite what Temporary Judge Coutts says, the practical reality is very much as is stated in *Jackson & Powell*. Perhaps the best summary is that given by Hugh Evans in his recent, and valuable, *Lawyers' Liabilities*:[3]

> As a general principle, the client's recollection is more likely to be correct, because for him the transaction is important and unusual, whereas for the solicitor it is one of hundreds of similar conveyances. However, each case depends on its own facts.

SERVITUDES

A view of the silage bales

Servitudes of prospect are rare, and litigation on such servitudes rarer still. *MacAlister v Wallace*[4] is the first such case for a number of years.[5] In 1947 the owner of land in Arran sold a part of the land on which a house stood. Among the servitudes conferred by the disposition was a:

> right to prevent the obstruction of the view from the front of the house known as Shedog House, erected on the subjects hereby disponed, to the south and south west by the erection of buildings or planting of trees on the portion of said remaining ground belonging to me . . . lying to the east of the line marked A B on the said plan annexed and subscribed as relative hereto. . . .

For many years the servitude was, it seems, forgotten about, and during this time trees were planted on the servient tenement which interfered with the view to the south and south east. In 2000 a stable block was planned for the property. At this point the servitude was rediscovered, and interdict sought on its basis.

In argument, and in the sheriff's judgment, the nature of a servitude of prospect was explored by reference to Roman law.[6] Arguably Roman law protected

1 Paragraph 19 of the opinion.
2 Paragraph 18 of the opinion.
3 2nd edn, 2002, at para 4-06.
4 Kilmarnock Sheriff Court, 25 June 2002, A1704/00 (unreported).
5 For an earlier example see *Matthews v Horne* (1974) *Unreported Cases from the Sheriff Courts* (eds R R M Paisley and D J Cusine, 2000) p 354.
6 Relying on Alan Rodger, *Owners and Neighbours in Roman Law* (1972) chap 4.

only views which were beautiful in some degree. A view that was not attractive did not satisfy the *utilitas* test, that is, the test that a servitude must be for the benefit of the dominant tenement. The sheriff[1] was prepared to accept that the position in Scots law was the same as in Roman law. But this posed a difficulty for the dominant proprietor. One of the main purposes of the litigation was to preserve the view of a stack of silage bales which were sited from time to time on a field which he owned. This was because of fears that children might play on them and cause damage. But was a silage bale a thing of beauty? The sheriff doubted that this could be so:

> What the pursuer wants is to be able to see his silage bales at the corner of his field where it adjoins the road to Blackwaterfoot. I cannot see that such could be called a prospect. It is not a view he requires to have all the time because the bales are not there all the time. It is not what may be called a pleasing prospect on any view. Such plastic-covered bales, which are now a common feature on farms, are not generally regarded as adding to the beauty of the countryside—rather the opposite. I cannot imagine that any prospective purchaser of the pursuer's property would take the view that they provide a view which would cause the value of the property to be enhanced. In my view what the pursuer desiderates does not meet the requirement of a *utilis* prospect.

Other, more winning, views which might have been available were already blocked for other reasons—principally by the pursuer's own trees or those of another neighbour who was not subject to the servitude—and so would not be adversely affected by the proposed building or the trees. No case for interdict or removal had therefore been made out.[2]

This decision may strike some as requiring more benefit (*utilitas*) than is warranted by the general law of servitudes. Further, it is debatable whether the difference between 'good' and 'not good' views is sufficiently objective to form a useful distinction in a question of real right.[3]

The decision is noteworthy in a number of other respects. First, some of the obstruction was caused not by trees but by shrubs. Only trees, however, were mentioned in the servitude. The court rejected the pursuer's argument that, as a matter of ordinary English, 'trees' included shrubs and that most people did not know the difference between them. Instead the servitude must be strictly construed, and a strict construction excluded shrubs. It may be noted here that, while servitudes are generally interpreted more leniently than real burdens,[4] a

1 Sheriff T M Croan.

2 The court also considered the issue on the basis (so far as we can follow the judgment) that the words imported a servitude *non aedificandi*. It is not clear why words which are tied to prospect should have a separate basis in another type of servitude; but in any event it was held that the proposed building was not, to any significant extent, within the area protected by the servitude. This conclusion was reached after a careful consideration of the direction of possible views looking south, and after distinguishing the different senses of north (true north, compass north, and grid north).

3 For a defence of this 'curiously un-legal' approach, see, however, Alan Rodger, *Owners and Neighbours in Roman Law* pp 129–131.

4 *Conveyancing 1999* pp 57–59.

negative servitude (such as prospect) closely resembles a real burden and tends to be subject to similar interpretative rules.[1] The court's decision is in line with this approach.

Secondly, the court was influenced by the pursuer's failure, over a number of years, to enforce the servitude in respect of the trees. Now it was too late for them to be cut down. This seems to be an example of acquiescence rather than, as the court would have it, a breach of the rule that a servitude must be exercised *civiliter*—a rule which seems to presuppose positive actings, and therefore to be confined to positive servitudes. Indeed more might have been made both of acquiescence, and also of negative prescription, which would have extinguished any breach of the servitude made more than 20 years ago.

Next, the court expressed scepticism about the pursuer's alternative crave for damages of £10,000. If there was a breach, the servitude could be enforced, by interdict and an order to remove trees and other obstructions. And if there was no breach, no damages were due. Despite this analysis, however, it is possible to envisage circumstances in which a remedy of damages might be appropriate. In particular, if a servient owner erects a building in breach of a servitude, a court might prefer to award damages than to require that the building be demolished.[2] In the, somewhat similar, case of encroachment the court has a discretion to make such an award even where it is not sought by the pursuer.[3] There seems no reason why the same principle should not apply to servitudes. Indeed another servitude case from 2002, *Thomas v Allan*,[4] is supportive of that principle. As the sheriff in *MacAlister* pointed out, however, a practical difficulty—which arises also with encroachment—is that some method of discharge would be needed if a successor of the pursuer were not to re-open the claim.

Finally, brief mention may be made of the position under the Title Conditions (Scotland) Bill, currently before the Scottish Parliament. When Part 7 of the Bill (once enacted) comes into force, on 28 November 2004, negative servitudes will disappear as a legal category. All existing negative servitudes will be converted into real burdens. Thereafter, any provision designed to protect light or prospect will require to be constituted as a real burden. The change is mainly directed at rules of constitution. There is little or no change as to the substance of the right. In particular, the rule that a servitude (in future a real burden) must confer benefit on the dominant tenement is preserved.[5]

Servitudes on public roads

Hamilton v Mundell; Hamilton v J & J Currie Ltd[6] concerned a public road running through the defenders' land but the *solum* of which, it was averred, belonged to

---

1 D J Cusine and R R M Paisley, *Servitudes and Rights of Way* (1998) para 3.34.
2 Quite often, of course, acquiescence would cure the breach, and the question of a remedy would not arise.
3 K G C Reid, *The Law of Property in Scotland* (1996) paras 178 and 423.
4 2002 GWD 12-368.
5 Title Conditions (Scotland) Bill, s 3(3).
6 Dumfries Sheriff Court, 20 November 2002, A578/01 and A591/01 (unreported).

the pursuer. In 1983 the road was stopped up, meaning, in the sheriff's view, that all public rights ceased.[1] Nonetheless the defenders continued to use the road for access. Just short of the prescriptive period of 20 years, possession was judicially interrupted by the raising of the present action. Naturally, predecessors of the defenders had used the road for many years prior to the stopping up, as a means of access to their land. That use, they argued, was sufficient to create a servitude by prescription.

The pursuer's counter-argument was simple but powerful. In order to qualify for the purposes of prescription, possession must be unequivocally referable to the right which it is sought to acquire. That principle is well-established.[2] It means, for example, that a person who possesses land as a tenant cannot found on that possession as the basis for the prescriptive acquisition of ownership or some other right.[3] Possession will be attributed to the lease and not to the putative new right. On the same basis, the defenders' possession in the present case was, and always had been, attributable to a public right. The same possession could not be used to found prescriptive acquisition of a servitude.

The sheriff,[4] having found that the authorities on this question as respects servitudes were sparse and equivocal, concluded that the defenders' argument 'accords with common sense' and allowed a proof of prescriptive possession. The decision has been appealed, and it would not be surprising if the appeal succeeds. The decision at first instance overlooks the principle that a person against whom prescription runs must have the opportunity of interruption; and that for such an opportunity to arise there must first be knowledge—or at least the possibility of knowledge—of the right which is being claimed. 'Only if the possessor openly possesses can a party whose interest is affected by the adverse possession be said to have had a fair chance to challenge the right asserted; only then, if he fails to challenge, can that party be said to have slept on his rights.'[5] On the present facts there was nothing which would have alerted the owner of the road to the claim of a servitude. Initially the possession was solely attributable to the public right.[6] At some later point, we are to suppose, it changed, so that in using the road the defenders' predecessors were claiming to exercise a servitude rather than a public right. But of this change there was no notice.[7] Use of the

1 There are difficult issues here about the relationship between public rights of passage and public rights of way. See *MacKinnon v Argyll and Bute Council* 2001 SLT 1275, discussed in *Conveyancing 2000* pp 49–51. The impression given by the legislation—now contained in Part VI of the Roads (Scotland) Act 1984—is that only pedestrian rights will survive stopping up. See 1984 Act, ss 68(4)(a) and 71(4). But the legislation does not in terms extinguish a public right of way, including a right for vehicles, which had previously been established by prescription.

2 D Johnston, *Prescription and Limitation* (1999) para 16.27.

3 *Houstoun v Barr* 1911 SC 134. See also Land Reform (Scotland) Act 2003, s 5(5).

4 Sheriff Kenneth Ross.

5 D Johnston, *Prescription and Limitation* para 16.15. And see also para 16.27.

6 The position might well be different where use on the basis of the servitude or purported servitude preceded the creation of the public right. See *McGavin v McIntyre* (1874) 1 R 1016.

7 The need for notice explains why a tenant cannot prescribe for ownership for as long as rent is still being paid. The non-payment of rent alerts the landlord to the changed basis of possession. See *Grant v Grant* (1677) Mor 10876.

road continued exactly as before. There was, in short, nothing which might have alerted the owner of the road to the need to challenge the possession.[1] Thus, if the sheriff is correct, the running of prescription was, for all practical purposes, unstoppable. The defenders' predecessors were *bound* to acquire the right. It seems unlikely that that is the law.

Conflicting servitudes and access for construction traffic

McMillan v Ghaly[2] is a reminder of the difficulties which can arise where a house is to be built on the dominant tenement. Both the pursuers and the defender acquired property from a common author in 1998. The defender's property was the west wing of a substantial house, and included an established driveway. The pursuers' property was a building plot. In terms of both sets of titles, the pursuers had a servitude of access over the defender's driveway for some, but not all, of its length. In the event, the contractors employed by the pursuers to build their house made some use of the 'wrong' part of the driveway, partly because of the difficulty of turning heavy vehicles, and partly because clear access had not yet been made available from the 'right' part of the driveway. The defender's protests went largely unheeded, and a draft agreement foundered when one of the pursuers refused to sign. For a number of weeks trespass took place on an almost daily basis, causing damage to the defender's garden and plants and to the surface of the driveway. And, in the words of the sheriff,[3] the defender had 'the misfortune of having to spend three months living in a house surrounded by mud'. The defender did not seek interdict at the time—as well he might have done—and the present litigation was largely concerned with damages for a trespass that had now largely ceased. Damages were awarded under the defender's counterclaim: (1) for repair of the surface damage to the 'wrong' part of the driveway; (2) for distress and inconvenience (£2,000); and (3) for the legal expenses of preparing the failed agreement.[4]

The case usefully illustrates a number of points. One is the importance, when purchasing a building plot, of ensuring that any access servitude is sufficient to allow the passage of construction traffic. This is partly a matter of the weight and frequency of such traffic, which may take the usage outwith an ordinary servitude of access.[5] For, typically, the surface of a driveway will be designed for light traffic only, and, as the sheriff pointed out in *McMillan*, 'it is a matter of simple physics that a vehicle weighing forty times that of the average motor car

1 Normally possession is challenged by interdict, but in the present case the defenders' predecessors were entitled to use the road in exercise of the public right, so that judicial interruption, by declarator, would have been necessary.

2 2002 GWD 30-1046.

3 Sheriff R A Davidson.

4 On this last point the sheriff noted that 'whatever may be the precise correct description of the legal obligation here, in my opinion equity demands that the pursuers reimburse the defender these costs'.

5 The problem may arise equally if, as sometimes, the driveway is held as common property. See *Mackay v Gaylor* 2001 GWD 1-59.

will have a significantly greater impact on a road surface than will that car'. In *McMillan* this issue sounded in damages only, for the wording of the servitude ('a heritable and irredeemable servitude right of vehicular and pedestrian access *for all purposes*') was sufficiently wide to allow the traffic in the first place.[1] Another difficulty, present in *McMillan*, is that heavy vehicles may require turning space which goes beyond the geographical limits of the servitude.

Secondly, the defender had reason to believe that further trespasses might occur. Accordingly he sought interdict. The sheriff, although sympathetic, refused interdict on the basis that the titles—which, on the evidence, were 'ineptly drafted'—did not accurately disclose the full extent of the servitude. The argument is a simple one. An interdict must properly indicate that which is forbidden. But this cannot be done if the boundary between the 'right' part of the driveway (ie that part which is subject to the servitude) and the 'wrong' part cannot be properly drawn. The result is logical, and yet unsatisfactory. The pursuers are protected by the vagueness of their own right, while the defender cannot protect his property against trespass. The answer presumably lies in an interdict which is more carefully drawn. For while the servitude was unclear at the margins, there were parts of the driveway which, incontestably, the servitude did not affect; and for those parts at least, an interdict would presumably be available.

The final point is best illustrated by an example. Suppose that in 1945 land was divided into two parts—plot A and plot B—and plot A sold. The disposition of plot A reserved a servitude right of way in favour of plot B. Later, in 1955, plot B was sold in turn. The disposition conferred a servitude right of way over plot A. Future purchasers of plot B will, in general, take the terms of the servitude from the 1955 disposition. Yet they are wrong to do so. The servitude was actually created by the reservation in the 1945 deed; and, insofar as the wording of the two deeds is different, the position is regulated by the 1945 deed. This is because the granter of the 1955 disposition no longer owned plot A and could not grant a *new* servitude over it. All that could be done was to make mention of a servitude *already constituted* by the disposition of 1945. This is a potential trap. Successive deeds are not always consistent in respect of servitudes; and a small difference in wording can make a large difference to the right which the servitude confers.

The difficulty arises only where the reservation *precedes* the grant. If the facts are reversed, the problem disappears. Thus suppose that the disposition granted in 1945 was of plot B and not of plot A. In that disposition there would be an express grant of the servitude. The 1955 disposition, of plot A, would then contain a matching reservation. Here the legal analysis is rather different. Unlike before, future purchasers of plot B can rely on the grant of the servitude, for it was by that grant that the right was created. Even if, therefore, the 1955 disposition failed to reserve a servitude—or reserved one but on less generous terms—the servitude exists by virtue of the 1945 deed. If, however, the 1955 disposition

---

1 See, on the phrase 'for all purposes', *Grant v Cameron* (1990) *Unreported Cases from the Sheriff Courts* (ed R R M Paisley and D J Cusine, 2000) p 264.

reserved a *higher* right, plot B takes the benefit of that right also. This is because, as owner of plot A, the granter of the 1955 disposition was free to burden it—even in a manner that went further than the original 1945 grant.

In summary, where the reservation of a servitude precedes the grant, the terms of the servitude are to be taken from the reservation alone. But where, conversely, the grant precedes the reservation, the grant can be augmented, but not diminished, by the terms of the subsequent reservation. That was what happened in *McMillan*. The grant and the reservation, although drawn up more or less contemporaneously, were not in precisely the same terms. In particular, while the grant referred merely to a 'servitude right of pedestrian and vehicular access', the reservation added the crucial words 'for all purposes'. The grant was recorded first. Nonetheless, the grant was augmented by the more expansive reservation, so that the pursuers were entitled to use 'for all purposes'.[1]

The first rule—that, where the order is (1) reservation and (2) grant, the terms of the servitude are to be taken from the reservation alone—is awkward in practice and, if taken seriously, would require purchasers to check the chronology of separation in respect of every grant of servitude. Happily, the problem disappears under registration of title. If a servitude appears in the property section of the dominant tenement, it may be taken that the servitude is good, and that further inquiry is unnecessary. The reasons why may be postponed until later.[2]

TRUSTS, LIFERENTS AND TAILZIES

Sales by trustees

Montagu Ninian Alexander Brodie, 25th Brodie of Brodie, of Brodie Castle, by Forres, transferred the castle, and certain other assets, to a family trust. This was in 1968. His son, Alastair Ian Ninian Brodie, was the beneficial liferenter. The son was getting married at that time, and the beneficial fee of the trust estate was destined to the latter's future issue. Three children were born of the marriage, Alexander, Phaedra and Edward-Benedict, who were the pursuers in the present action. By 1978 the son's marriage had broken up. He went to Australia and his wife, with the three young children, went to France. At this stage the trustees (one of whom was the truster) sold the castle to the Secretary of State (the first defender). The sale was without the consent of the beneficial liferenter, following the advice of senior counsel. The Secretary of State bought the castle with the intention of transferring it to the National Trust for Scotland (the second defender), which was duly done in 1980. The contents of the castle had never been transferred to the trust, but the truster sold them to the Secretary of State, who transferred them to the National Trust for Scotland. It seems that the truster

1 This issue was not, however, argued in the case.
2 They are discussed below at pp 83–84.

donated the proceeds of the sale of the contents to the National Trust for Scotland to form a maintenance endowment for the castle.

Eventually the three children grew up. They felt that they had been unfairly deprived of their patrimony. In 1999 there were media reports that Alexander was evicted from the castle by sheriff officers, and there had already been a history of litigation in the family.[1] Eventually, as party litigants, the children raised the present action: *Brodie v Secretary of State for Scotland*.[2] They convened a variety of defenders, including their grandfather, by now about 90 years of age,[3] the Secretary of State, and the National Trust for Scotland. They had a variety of conclusions, including one for reduction of the title and the revesting of the castle in the family trust. One of the averments was that the 1978 sale had been at less than fair value.

The action was dismissed as irrelevant. It is not without interest from a conveyancing standpoint. In the first place, whilst Lady Smith's opinion gives no details of the terms of the trust deed, it is likely that a power of sale, unfettered by the need for the consent of any beneficiary, existed. Although the fact is not always appreciated, trustees almost invariably have a power of sale, and the fact that the trust estate is subject to a beneficial liferent normally makes no difference.[4]

The case also illustrates a point of trust law that is often not appreciated, namely the effect of s 2 of the Trusts (Scotland) Act 1961. This rather mysterious provision says that if trustees sell trust property then 'the validity of the transaction and of any title acquired by the second party [ie the purchaser] under the transaction shall not be challengeable by the second party or any other person on the ground that the act in question is at variance with the terms or purposes of the trust'. Since a person who bought from trustees in good faith was protected at common law anyway, the effect of the statutory provision seems to be—and has generally been understood as being—that purchasers in *bad faith* are protected, a remarkable result. Given that s 2 is an important provision passed four decades ago, it is curious that, so far as we are aware, it has hitherto not been the subject of judicial consideration. Its effect in the present case was that, even if the original sale had been in breach of trust, and even if the purchaser, the Secretary of State, was in bad faith, nevertheless the pursuers would not be able to obtain the remedy of reduction.

Cautio usufructuaria

What happens if there is a proper liferent, and the liferenter is thought by the fiar to be neglecting the property, allowing it to fall into disrepair? The question does not often arise, for the simple reason that proper liferents are uncommon. But it arose in *Stronach's Exrs v Robertson*,[5] and its resolution

1 *The Guardian*, 17 March 1999.
2 2002 GWD 20-698.
3 He died on 3 March 2003.
4 Cf *Mauchline Ptr* 1992 SLT 421.
5 2002 SLT 1044, 2002 SCLR 843.

necessitated deep study of old cases, old statutes, the institutional writers, and Roman law itself.

In 1971 a house at 6 Hillside Road, Stromness, Orkney, was conveyed to James P Robertson in liferent and to his sister Eleanor Robertson in fee. Eventually the fiar died, and the fee thus passed to her estate. Her executors, concerned about the state of the property, raised an action against the liferenter, narrating a sad story of dilapidation, and seeking decree requiring the defender to carry out specified repairs, which failing to pay damages to the pursuers. Given that a liferenter is bound to take reasonable care of the subjects, the pursuers apparently had a stateable case.

The defender came up with a simple but powerful defence. Where there is a proper liferent, the fiar's remedy against the liferenter is to demand that the liferenter find caution, known as liferent caution, or, in Latin, as *cautio usufructuaria*. The adoption of the Roman rule is generally ascribed to the Liferent Caution Act 1491 and the Liferent Caution Act 1535, but it is arguable that the rule is in fact a common law one. On this issue the case was fought out, and the defender won both in Kirkwall Sheriff Court and in the First Division. Presumably the pursuers will now raise a new action, on Roman lines. Lady Paton, giving the judgment of the court, helpfully offered some advice as to how this should be done:[1]

> If decree ordaining the respondent to lodge caution were granted, and if there were failure on the part of the respondent to obtemper that decree, the usual forms of diligence could be considered. Another compulsitor might be the forfeiture of the 'fruits' of the estate (1535 Act; Erskine II.9.59; Stair's *Institutes* II.6.4). However, forfeiture of the fruits might be of limited assistance in the context of a residential dwellinghouse, unless it could be argued that one of the fruits should, in the twenty-first century, be regarded as including the actual right to occupy. A further form of compulsitor might be contempt of court.

We offer two footnotes to this passage. One is that it is perhaps not clear what sort of diligence would be available to enforce a decree ordering caution to be found. The other footnote concerns 'forfeiture of "fruits"'. The actual term does not occur in any of the three authorities cited (the 1535 Act, Stair or Erskine), though Dobie uses it in his summary of the 1535 Act.[2] Even if the 1535 Act had used that expression, it would not, arguably, have given rise to any difficulty of interpretation. The term 'fruits' comes from *fructus* and can have the broad meaning of that word, which is 'enjoyment' or 'benefit' or 'profit'.[3] A liferenter has the *ususfructus*, and loss of the fruits simply means loss of the *ususfructus*. If the *ususfructus* takes the form of actual occupation, then actual occupation is what the liferenter loses (until such time as caution is found).

The rule of Roman law was that a liferenter (the usufructuary) who failed to find caution lost the enjoyment of the property to the fiar (*dominus*) until such

---

1 2002 SLT 1044 at 1053E.
2 W J Dobie, *Manual of the Law of Liferent and Fee* (1941) p 244.
3 The root verb is *fruor, fruere*.

time as caution was found. This was also our common law, assuming (what is uncertain) that this area of law was received as a matter of common law, rather than by means of the 1491 Act. But the 1535 Act makes a strange alteration, in that it provides that the benefit of a forfeited liferent passes, not to the fiar, but—remarkably—to the Crown. The logic is baffling, but the wording seems clear enough, and whilst the 1535 Act has been amended, most recently in 1964,[1] the part about the Crown's rights stands in 2003 as it stood in 1535. Stair notices the point, but Erskine does not: he merely states, in the passive, that the liferenter is 'excluded from the yearly profits of the subjects liferented till security be given'.[2] Nor do later writers seem to notice this part of the 1535 Act. In the passage quoted above the court does not say in whose favour the temporary forfeiture would operate, but if they had the Crown in mind one would have expected the passage to have been worded rather differently. Possibly this strange provision in the 1535 Act is precisely the reason why liferent caution is so rare in practice, for whilst the liferenter would suffer by his defiance, the fiar would not gain. However, if we are correct in our speculation that the Roman law of liferent caution forms part of Scots common law, the 1491 and 1535 Acts being merely declaratory of and supplementary to the common law, then it becomes possible to argue that the 1535 Act merely confers an *option* on the Crown, and that if the Crown does not seek to exercise that option (and nowadays it would no doubt not seek to do so) then the fiar's common law rights (which are his rights in the civil law) stand whole and entire. No doubt the action of forfeiture would have to call the Lord Advocate for his interest.

The whole subject of repairs as between liferenter and fiar is complex and obscure, and it is no criticism of this valuable decision to say that even now a good deal of obscurity remains. It is important to observe that the pursuers sought specific implement, which failing damages, and the decision is limited to those attempted remedies. We now know certain possibilities were *not* open to the pursuers, and we now know one possibility that *was* open to them: *cautio usufructuria*. As to *other* possible remedies, such as (1) the appointment of a judicial factor, (2) warrant to the fiars to execute necessary repairs themselves with the liferenter bound to contribute an equitable share of the expense, or (3) damages against the liferenter's estate at the expiry of the liferent, it is still possible to speculate, and there is in the old authorities plenty of material available for quarrying.

Finally, the case reinforces the traditional view that improper (trust) liferents are to be preferred to proper ones.

Trusts, liferents and quasi-entails

Arthur James Balfour was born in East Lothian in 1848, the year of the Entail Amendment (Scotland) Act, which for the first time provided machinery whereby entails (tailzies) could be broken. After Eton and Cambridge, he pursued a

1 Statute Law Revision (Scotland) Act 1964.
2 Erskine II.9.59.

successful political career, which came to a climax in 1902, when he succeeded his uncle, Lord Salisbury, as Prime Minister. He demitted office in 1905. Later, as Foreign Secretary in the coalition government, he was the author of the well-known Balfour Declaration about the future of Palestine. Since he was a Tory one imagines that he would have voted against the Entail (Scotland) Bill which was passed in 1914 under the Liberal administration. This Act prohibited the creation of any new strict entails. In 1922 he was ennobled as the First Earl of Balfour. He never married.

In his old age he decided that his lands in East Lothian should be entailed to his brother, Gerald William Balfour, who would become the Second Earl, and then to Gerald's heirs male, in perpetuity, whom failing to his other brother, Eustace James Anthony Balfour, and to Eustace's heirs male, in perpetuity. In the event of complete failure of heirs male, heirs female would succeed. But because of the 1914 Act, he could not do this directly. So he attempted to achieve the same effect by an alternative route. His trust disposition and settlement conveyed his estate to trustees, who were to hold for behoof of these successive heirs, each successive heir having a beneficial liferent. Title would remain vested perpetually in the trustees, and so this would not, strictly speaking, be an entail at all, though its substantive effect would be much the same.[1] The trust disposition and settlement was dated 1923. A codicil of 1927 made a variation purely for tax reasons: the first beneficiary would not be Gerald, but Gerald's son, the future Third Earl.

Arthur Balfour died in 1930. All then went according to plan. When the Third Earl—the First Earl's nephew—died in 1968 the beneficial interest passed to his son, the Fourth Earl, Gerald Arthur Balfour, the petitioner in the present case.[2] The Fourth Earl now wished to break the quasi-entail, and take the lands for himself absolutely. In this plan he was opposed by his cousin, Roderick Francis Arthur Balfour. One guesses that the latter was the heir male of Eustace and also the next beneficiary who would take on the death of the Fourth Earl, though these points are not expressly covered in the reports of the case.

Could the Fourth Earl break the quasi-entail? And did his great-uncle's trust disposition and settlement successfully circumvent the legislation?

The Entail Amendment (Scotland) Act 1848[3] provided machinery for disentailing land. By s 47:

> where any land ... shall by virtue of any ... deed of trust ... be in the lawful possession of a party of full age born after the date of such ... deed of trust, such party shall not be in any way affected by any ... conditions ... in such ... deed of trust ... being of the nature of ... conditions ... of entail or intended to regulate the succession of such party ...

1 The deed provided for the beneficial fee, but this was no doubt for form's sake, because the chance that the fee would ever vest was evidently minimal.

2 *Earl of Balfour Ptr* 2002 SLT 981 *rev* 2002 SLT 1385.

3 11 & 12 Vict c 38, commonly called the Rutherford Act.

In such circumstances the party may apply for an order vesting the property absolutely in him, such order to be recorded in the Sasine Register. The next section, s 48, provided that 'it shall be competent to grant an estate limited to a liferent interest in favour only of a party in life at the date of such grant' and further providing that a breach of that rule would authorise the liferenter for the time being to apply to the Court of Session for a vesting order, as under s 47. Section 47 is still in force, as is s 48, though the latter now only applies to pre-1968 deeds, being replaced for post-1968 deeds by s 18 of the Law Reform (Miscellaneous Provisions) (Scotland) Act 1968. No doubt the First Earl's legal advisers knew of these provisions. The First Earl's hope was, one supposes, that no future heir would seek to invoke them.

The Fourth Earl presented a petition to the Court of Session for an order vesting the lands in himself absolutely, founding on both s 47 and s 48. But to be successful he had to show that he was 'born after the date of such . . . deed of trust'. There was no dispute as to his date of birth, which was in 1925. But was the year 1925 before or after the deed of trust? The deed itself was dated 1923, but the codicil was dated 1927. A good case could be made for saying that the Fourth Earl had not been alive when his great-uncle made the deed, since the core provisions of the quasi-entail were in the 1923 deed. And an equally good case could be made for saying the opposite, on the ground that a testamentary deed and its codicils must be read together, and if a single date has to be ascribed to them—an artificial exercise but one necessitated by the wording of the 1848 Act—it has to be the later date, since to take the earlier date would be to take the date of a deed which, as such, never took effect.

The case could have been decided either way, and it was. The Inner House held that the relevant date was 1927, so that the Fourth Earl's petition must fail. The Earl appealed to the House of Lords, which took the opposite view, holding that 1923 was the relevant date, with the result that the petition succeeded. In fact the most logical date would have been the date of death, 1930, but that possibility was excluded by previous case law on the 1848 Act.

It may be added that such proper entails as still remain (all created before the 1914 Act) will be extinguished on 28 November 2004 by s 50 of the Abolition of Feudal Tenure etc (Scotland) Act 2000.

REGISTRATION OF TITLE

Servitudes and the curative effect

The treatment of servitudes under registration of title is complex and, to some extent, uncertain. The difficulty is caused by the rule of the general law which allows a servitude to be created off the Register, whether by prescription or by implied grant. The result is that servitudes may exist even though the Register is silent.

So far as the *servient* tenement is concerned, the Land Registration (Scotland) Act 1979 accommodates the difficulty by making servitudes into overriding interests. This means that servitudes may, or may not, be disclosed on the Register; but even where not disclosed they bind the land.[1]

The position is much the same for the *dominant* tenement, although the label 'overriding interest' is not appropriate here. In recent years the Keeper has abandoned the previous, and generous, practice of including prescriptive servitudes on the Register on evidence of possession, experience having shown that such evidence may not tell the whole story. Now a servitude alleged to have been created by prescription will be included only where it has been judicially declared.[2] The effect is that servitudes quite often do not appear on the title sheet of the dominant tenement. On the other hand, where they do appear, they take the benefit of the usual rules of land registration, and in particular of the 'curative' effect of s 3(1) of the 1979 Act.[3]

Marshall v Duffy[4] was a case where a servitude did appear on the title sheet of the dominant tenement.[5] But, or so it was argued, the grant was *a non domino*. The facts were rather unusual. An area of land, which was the dominant tenement in a servitude of way,[6] was divided into three plots. In the disposition of the first plot to be sold (which we may call 'plot A'), the servitude was repeated, but the granter and his successors 'as proprietors of the subjects retained by him' were expressly excluded from future access over the road. The effect of this formula is unclear, but on one view it amounted to a discharge of the servitude *quoad* plots B and C.[7] If so, the servitude was now restricted to plot A, and could not be included in any subsequent conveyance of plots B and C. In fact the servitude *was* included in the conveyance of plot C (though not of plot B), and duly appeared on the title sheet of that plot. What was the effect?

Section 3(1)(a) of the 1979 Act provides that, on registration of an interest in land, the interest vests together with 'a real right in and to . . . any right, pertinent or servitude, express or implied, forming part of the interest'. In the present case the servitude was expressed on the title sheet; and since, by virtue of s 3(1)(a), title comes from the Register and not from the underlying deed, it did not matter that the deed might have been inept to create the servitude. Hence, it was held, a servitude was duly created on registration. The curative principle is a familiar one, but *Marshall* marks the first occasion on which it has been applied in the context of servitudes. The decision should reassure purchasers of land in cases where access is dependent on a servitude. For provided that the servitude appears on the land certificate (and title sheet), its existence is established as a matter of law.

---

1 Land Registration (Scotland) Act 1979, ss 3(1)(a) and 28(1).
2 *Registration of Title Practice Book* paras 6.54–6.58.
3 Ie the rule that registration cures any defect in the deed inducing registration.
4 2002 GWD 10-318.
5 It is not clear from the judgment whether it appeared in the property section or in the burdens section. Nor is it clear, as a matter of law, whether anything turns on the difference.
6 Or so it was assumed in the litigation. In fact the wording of the grant seems more consistent with common property: 'a joint and mutual right with the proprietors of the remaining lands of East Overton . . . to the service or access road'.
7 In fact the court was not addressed on this point, and Lord Philip (at para 24) expressly reserved his opinion as to whether successors of the granter were excluded.

Servitudes and proprietors in possession

That, however, is not quite the end of the story. A servitude which requires the aid of s 3(1)(a) of the Land Registration (Scotland) Act 1979 is one which should not have been entered in the first place. The Register, in other words, is inaccurate. And where the Register is inaccurate, it is possible that it may be rectified, under s 9 of the 1979 Act, to the effect of having the servitude deleted. In the event of rectification, the dominant proprietor would usually be entitled to indemnity from the Keeper, but the servitude would be lost.

In practice, of course, the question of whether rectification can or cannot take place depends on whether the dominant proprietor is a proprietor in possession. For by s 9(3) of the Act, the Register cannot usually be rectified against such a proprietor. A purchaser who, in relation to a servitude, is a proprietor in possession is therefore substantially free from the risk of rectification. But while the rule is clear what is less clear is the manner in which a servitude holder can become a proprietor in possession. This issue was considered, but not in the end decided, by *Mutch v Mavisbank Properties Ltd*.[1]

There was some previous authority. In the leading case of *Kaur v Singh*[2] the First Division distinguished, in effect, between real rights which command their own title sheet—principally ownership and long lease—and real rights which do not. The holder of a right of the first kind is a 'proprietor' in the sense of s 9(3). A holder of a right of the second kind—the particular right considered in *Kaur* was a standard security—is not. This means that a heritable creditor, for example, can never be a proprietor in possession and so is not protected against rectification.

Servitudes do not command their own title sheet. Yet in one important respect they are different from standard securities or other subordinate real rights. Subordinate real rights are usually freestanding. A servitude, however, can only be held by the owner of other land. It is, in other words, a pertinent of ownership. This means that it stands between the two rules articulated in *Kaur v Singh*. The holder of a servitude is not, *qua* servitude, a 'proprietor' in the sense of s 9(3), any more than a heritable creditor is such a proprietor. But a servitude can only be held in association with ownership, that is to say, as a pertinent of the dominant land, and *qua* owner of the dominant land the servitude holder is plainly a 'proprietor'. In *Mutch v Mavisbank Properties Ltd* the sheriff principal chose to emphasise the fact of ownership:[3]

> I am rather inclined to the view that in a case where the Keeper is being asked to rectify the Register by deleting a servitude right of access from the title sheet, a dominant proprietor would in normal circumstances be 'prejudiced' and would as a matter of parliamentary intention fall to be regarded as a 'proprietor in possession'.

This approach receives support both from the language of s 9(3) itself—for removal of the servitude would indeed be to the prejudice of 'a' proprietor in

1 2002 SLT (Sh Ct) 91. Another aspect of this case is considered at p 87.
2 1999 SC 180.
3 2002 SLT (Sh Ct) 91 at 94I per Sheriff Principal E F Bowen QC.

possession[1]—and also from the fact that s 3(1)(a) ties the acquisition of the servitude to the acquisition of ownership. But the sheriff principal's remarks were *obiter* and the position must be regarded as still in doubt.[2]

It seems reasonable to assume that 'proprietorship', once established, determines possession—or in other words, that one must possess that of which, in terms of s 9(3), one is a qualifying proprietor. As applied to servitudes, this would mean possession of the dominant tenement rather than possession of the servitude itself. Nonetheless in *Mutch* the sheriff principal seems to have assumed that it was the servitude which required to be possessed.[3]

Errors of transcription

The divergence between title sheet and underlying deed may occur in small matters as well as great. A standard small matter is an error of transcription. Such an error may take different forms.[4] Words present in the deed may be omitted from the Register. Or words may be added which are not found in the original deed. Or again the words may be rearranged or changed in such a way as to make a change in meaning. Often such small differences go undetected. One of the benefits of registration of title, after all, is that it is normally unnecessary to look behind the Register, and so earlier deeds are not usually consulted. But if a particular entry comes under scrutiny, it is often helpful to look at the deed from which it came, in order to gain some idea of context, and of the overall use of language. Sometimes this will expose small differences in wording. But even if, as usually, the words were faithfully transcribed from deed to Register, the deed may be of assistance in matters of interpretation. *Marshall v Duffy*[5] considers, for the first time, whether such assistance is permissible.

In *Marshall* there was a difference in wording. The deed excluded access to a road by the granter and his successors as proprietors of 'the subjects retained by him'. The Register substituted 'East Overton House and ground and others'. On the basis that the difference was material, it was argued that the entry on the Register should be read in the light of the words used in the deed. This Lord Philip emphatically refused to do:[6]

> [T]he purpose of the Land Registration (Scotland) Act 1979 was to provide a title guaranteed to be valid by an indemnity from the Keeper of the Register. The intention was that the Register should be the only measure of the title and that it should contain

1 Ie the owner of the dominant tenement.

2 Even if the sheriff principal is right in a case, like *Mutch*, where the servitude is entered on the title sheet of the dominant tenement, the position might be different where it appears only on the title sheet of the servient tenement, on the basis that the 'proprietor' in question is then the servient owner and not the dominant, and there is no prejudice.

3 2002 SLT (Sh Ct) 91 at 94J. Similarly, the background facts to *Dougbar Properties Ltd v Keeper of the Registers of Scotland* 1999 SC 513 disclose that the Keeper rectified the Register to delete a leasehold 'servitude', apparently on the basis that there was no possession of the servitude.

4 Sometimes, of course, the 'error' is deliberate, or at least conscious, in the sense that a decision is taken to render certain words from the deed in a slightly different, and it may be shorter, way.

5 2002 GWD 10-318, discussed at pp 83–84 above on a different point.

6 Paragraphs 21 and 22.

> all the information relevant to the particular heritable interest . . . The entries in the Register represent the definitive measure of the parties' rights . . . In the absence of any conclusion for reduction or rectification of the titles, there is no justification for going behind the terms of these titles. To do so would defeat the purpose of the 1979 Act.

Lord Philip's view does not amount to saying that the Register is infallible. Usually a discrepancy means an inaccuracy, and an inaccuracy can in principle be rectified under s 9 of the 1979 Act.[1] But in the typical case, rectification would prejudice a proprietor in possession and so can only proceed in limited circumstances, such as where the inaccuracy was caused by the proprietor's fraud or carelessness.

Marshall was a case of difference in wording. Where the Register says one thing and the deed something else, the position, on the authority of *Marshall*, is to be governed by the Register alone. One may speculate that the rule may be different where the wording is identical[2] and the deed is being referred to only for its interpretative value. The problem here is what may be called the Humpty-Dumpty effect. By its very nature, registration of title tends to break deeds into pieces, and to display the pieces in a different order, and with omissions, in the land certificate. Nor is the provenance always disclosed, so that it may not be possible to tell that wording given in, say, the property section comes from the same deed as a later entry in the burdens section. In order to arrive at a sensible interpretation of a tricky phrase, it is often necessary to put the pieces back together again, and that can be done only by looking at the deed as a whole. Indeed if recourse to the original document is not permissible, it would mean that words used—and rights conferred—in a Sasine deed are vulnerable to a change of meaning when they are extracted and scattered, on first registration, in the Land Register.

Marshall deserves mention for one other reason which is unconnected with registration of title. Deed plans are rare in the law reports, although *Mactaggart & Co v Roemmele*[3]—which shows the feuing plan of Kelvinside Gardens in Glasgow—is a handsome exception. In *Marshall* Lord Philip makes frequent reference to a plan to explain the, otherwise incomprehensible, facts of the case; and the plan itself is reproduced, in full colour, on the Scottish Courts website.[4] This is an idea which deserves to catch on.

WARRANDICE

Mutch v Mavisbank Properties Ltd[5] is a reminder, if one is needed, of the importance of picking up title errors before settlement, or at least before the missives are

---

1 Indeed s 6(2) of the 1979 Act presupposes that what appears in the Register may be wrong.
2 Or at least where the difference is not being founded on, as such.
3 1907 SC 1318.
4 See www.scotcourts.gov.uk/opinions/PHI0502A.html.
5 2002 SLT (Sh Ct) 91. Another aspect of this case is discussed at p 85.

replaced by the disposition. Most title errors are covered by the 'good and marketable title' clause of the missives.[1] But quite often they are not covered by the warrandice clause in the disposition. This is because warrandice is typically a protection against eviction rather than against title error.[2] A purchaser, therefore, has no claim merely because the title is bad. That is just something which has to be put up with. A claim arises only where there is eviction—where, in other words, a third party with a better title enforces that title against the purchaser. Usually eviction means full judicial eviction, ie a decree against the purchaser. But sometimes less will do, such as the settling of an action in which the pursuer's success was inevitable. However, there can be no eviction without a third party intent on enforcing his or her rights. If, notwithstanding the defect in title, the purchaser is left undisturbed, there is no eviction, and so, in the typical case, no breach of warrandice and no ground for a claim. On one view, of course, that is fair enough, for enjoyment of the property is not at issue. But a title which is bad is also one which is unmarketable—unless of course the next purchaser also happens to overlook the defect. Otherwise the property can be enjoyed but not, in practice, sold.

Mutch is of interest because of the interaction of warrandice with the principles of registration of title. The facts were these. The pursuer bought a pub in Airdrie. The title sheet followed the disposition in including servitudes of pedestrian access to entrances at the side and rear of the bar. The side door was of particular importance as this was used as a fire exit. The pursuer was not left in peace for long. The owners of the land over which access was taken disputed the existence of the servitudes on grounds which, the pursuer alleged, were irresistible.[3] In those circumstances the pursuer made a temporary arrangement with the owners, so that the fire exit could continue in use, and then set to work creating a new fire exit. In this action he sought £70,000 from the sellers as damages for breach of warrandice.

The action was dismissed. It was possible, although not certain, that the owners' claim might have constituted eviction in the case of a Sasine title. But it did not constitute eviction in the case of a Land Register title. Whether the servitudes were fundamentally good or bad, the fact is that they had been included in the title sheet of the pub. Thus by s 3(1)(a) of the Land Registration (Scotland) Act 1979 any deficiency in their constitution was cured. Unless or until the Register was rectified, on the application of the neighbouring owners, the servitudes were good and could be enforced against those owners. And rectification would be refused if the pursuers were proprietors in possession.[4] It was argued for the defenders that, in a Land Register case, eviction must always include rectification of the Register, and indeed there is much to be said for this

1 G L Gretton and K G C Reid, *Conveyancing* (2nd edn, 1999) chap 6.
2 Typically but not always. In particular eviction is not required in respect of the warranties against subordinate real rights or unusual title conditions. See K G C Reid, *The Law of Property in Scotland* (1996) para 707.
3 They are not, however, specified in the report.
4 Land Registration (Scotland) Act 1979, s 9(3).

view. The sheriff principal, however, was not willing to go so far. But, at the least, 'the statutory effect of registration strengthens the need for clear averments as to the nature of a challenge'.[1] In the present case the nature of the third party's challenge was not properly set out.

COMPANY SECURITIES

Abolition of receivership

There is a legislative tradition that any given statute should be confined to one particular theme, whether it is a large theme, such as the Companies Act 1985, or a small theme, such as the Term and Quarter Days (Scotland) Act 1990. But for political and other reasons this tradition is not always adhered to. The Enterprise Act 2002 is about competition law. But it also contains legislative provisions on a quite different theme: receivership. Receivership is to be abolished. These provisions apply on both sides of the border.

Fashion is by its nature changeable: fashion in law is so too. Back in 1972 the English institution of receivership was so admired in Scotland that it was thought essential to introduce it: this was done by the Companies (Floating Charges and Receivers) (Scotland) Act 1972.[2] Thirty years later it is decided that receivership is, after all, a bad institution which must be abolished. One procedural difference is that whereas its introduction in 1972 was based on decision-making in Scotland, its abolition in 2002 was a London-based decision.

Law reform is sometimes deficient in rationality, and neither the introduction of receivership nor its abolition is easy to explain to the intelligent law student. Receivership always was an odd institution. We have grown used to it: foreigners regard it with astonishment. It seems to them remarkable that a creditor should be able to take over a company in this way. A receivership is rather like spirit possession: the company is possessed by the spirit. It seems that the company is acting, but it is the receiver acting, and the company's board of directors look on, powerless. Indeed, there can be several receivers in office simultaneously—multiple spirit possession. Even more remarkable, there can be simultaneous receivership and liquidation. Everyone knows that floating charges have created technical problems, not least in the field of property law: *Sharp v Thomson*[3] is but one example. And yet one might say that the problems have been caused only in part by the floating charge: what has really made things difficult has been the existence of receivership. Its abolition will make some things easier for the conveyancer.

The provisions on receivership are contained in sections 248 to 255 of the 2002 Act, amending the Companies Act 1985. They are not yet in force but it is

1 2002 SLT (Sh Ct) 91 at 94E per Sheriff Principal E F Bowen QC.
2 Based on the Scottish Law Commission's *Report on the Companies (Floating Charges) (Scotland) Act 1961* (Scot Law Com no 14, 1970).
3 1995 SC 455, *rev* 1997 SC (HL) 66. For a discussion, see pp 92–97 below.

expected that they will be brought into force before the end of 2003. The abolition will only affect floating charges created after the new provisions come into force. Thus if NewCo Ltd granted a floating charge to BankCo plc in 2002, and gets into financial difficulties in 2012, the bank will still be able to put it into receivership—assuming that by 2012 there have not been further changes in the law. Thus receivership will be around for many years to come, and it will be necessary to get used to distinguishing between 'pre-Act' and 'post-Act' floating charges. In addition, the provisions will not apply to six classes of post-Act floating charges. The definitions are complex, and will not even be summarised here, but the six classes are: (1) capital market charges; (2) public-private partnership charges; (3) utilities charges; (4) project finance charges; (5) financial market charges; and (6) registered social landlord charges. Why these six exceptions exist is not clear. It may be that the creative commercial lawyer will be able to exploit them in the future.

At the same time, the provisions make two other changes. They abolish Crown preference in company insolvencies, while at the same time improving the position of the ordinary unsecured creditors in relation to floating charges. This idea was recommended by the celebrated Cork Report[1] in 1980 but has taken 22 years to implement.

In the second place, certain changes are made to the law of company administration. For an essential feature of the new legislation is that it is intended to boost the use of administration. The idea is that administration, which at the moment is not very common, will in a few years be as common as receivership is now. Some quite radical changes are made to the law. One change is that the holder of a 'qualifying' floating charge will be able to appoint an administrator. Since most creditors will, no doubt, wish their floating charges to be 'qualifying' ones, and since the question of whether a floating charge 'qualifies ' depends to some extent on how it is drafted, the statutory provision is worth quoting:[2]

> (1) The holder of a qualifying floating charge in respect of a company's property may appoint an administrator of the company.
>
> (2) For the purposes of sub-paragraph (1) a floating charge qualifies if created by an instrument which—
>
> (a) states that this paragraph applies to the floating charge,
>
> (b) purports to empower the holder of the floating charge to appoint an administrator of the company,
>
> (c) purports to empower the holder of the floating charge to make an appointment which would be the appointment of an administrative receiver within the meaning given by section 29(2), or
>
> (d) purports to empower the holder of a floating charge in Scotland to appoint a receiver who on appointment would be an administrative receiver.

1 *Report of the Review Committee on Insolvency Law and Practice* (1980, Cmnd 8558).

2 Enterprise Act 2002, Sch 16, para 14. (This will take effect as a new Sch B1 to the Insolvency Act 1986.) For complete details the Act itself must be consulted.

Conveyancers need to keep an eye on the commencement date for the new provisions, for it will make a difference to clients whether floating charges are subject to the old or the new regime. The new legislation, when in force, will have an impact on refinancing packages. At present a floating charge in favour of Bank X can be discharged and replaced by another in favour of Bank Y, and apart from possible issues of ranking the effect of the two charges will be the same. But in the future such a refinancing would mean that the new floating charge would be rather different in its legal effect from the old floating charge.

It might be worthwhile for someone to create a store of ready-made companies all with pre-Act floating charges in place. These companies would be like a wine-cellar: one of them could be brought up from the cellar as and when needed. But the time available to create such a store is limited.

Registration

In most countries the requirements for creating a security over land are the same regardless of whether the granter is a company or a natural person. And once upon a time that was also true in Scotland. In either case the heritable security was recorded in the General Register of Sasines, and that was that. But in 1961 floating charges were introduced—by the Companies (Floating Charges) (Scotland) Act 1961. What has that to do with the creation of heritable securities? The logical answer is 'nothing at all'. But logic and legislation do not always walk together. It was decided that when a company grants a heritable security, that security must in future be recorded not only in the Register of Sasines (or now the Land Register) but also in the new Charges Register which was set up for the registration of floating charges. No reason was given for this innovation, which was borrowed from England. At one time in England neither floating charges nor mortgages (ie heritable securities) had to be registered at all. About 100 years ago it was decided to remedy this problem—but only for company debtors. Thus mortgages granted by companies were registered in the Charges Register, because that was the only place they could be registered.[1] When the floating charge was introduced to Scotland, the fact that heritable securities had to be recorded anyway meant that there was no need to require them to registered *also* in the Charges Register. Yet what happened was that the English legislation was simply copied. The result was that since 1961 heritable securities by companies have to be registered twice,[2] on pain of nullity.[3] The registration in the Charges Register has to be within 21 days of the registration in the Land or Sasine Register. It is all too easy to forget about the second registration. Because of Murphy's law, one can predict that if the second registration *has* been carried out the company will thrive (and so the bank will be paid off), but if it has *not*

1 Except in Yorkshire and Middlesex, which had recording systems somewhat similar to the Register of Sasines.

2 Actually they have to be registered three times, but the third registration, which is in the company's own 'internal' register, is less important.

3 The legislation is currently contained in ss 410–424 of the Companies Act 1985.

been made then the company is doomed. And then the bank will look to the law firm in question to compensate it for its losses.

The Scottish Law Commission has now produced a paper on the subject: *Discussion Paper on Registration of Rights in Security by Companies.*[1] It seeks views of consultees, but provisionally recommends that standard securities granted by companies should no longer have to be registered in the Charges Register: registration in the Land or Sasine Register will suffice, as with borrowers who are natural persons. If this comes to pass, it will be a victory for common sense, and certainly welcome news for conveyancers.

Under the current rules, it is not only floating charges and standard securities that have to be registered in the Charges Register. So must certain other types of security right, including securities over ships, over aircraft, and over intellectual property rights. The Commission's proposals would apply equally in such cases. In future only floating charges would be registrable at Companies House.

One other aspect of the Law Commission's proposals deserves mention. Under current law, a floating charge has to be registered within 21 days of its execution, but it comes into force at an earlier date, namely the date when the deed is delivered to the creditor.[2] There is thus a period of up to 21 days in which a floating charge may exist without any means by which third parties can know of it. The Commission provisionally recommends the abolition of the rule. The new rule would be that a floating charge simply comes into being when it is registered. This would also remove the strange rule that a floating charge cannot be registered after the expiry of the 21-day period.

PASSING OF PROPERTY

The legacy of *Sharp v Thomson*

Sharp v Thomson[3] concerned the problem of insolvency and the incomplete transaction. In that case a disposition of land had been delivered but not yet registered when the sellers went into receivership and a floating charge over their whole property and undertaking crystallised. The question at issue was whether the floating charge caught the land. On a traditional analysis of property law, the answer was yes. For without registration, the land remained the property of the sellers. Hence it was subject to the floating charge. The House of Lords, however, reversing the Court of Session,[4] applied a different rule. According to their Lordships, delivery of the disposition was in itself a crucial event. No doubt it did not pass ownership in the technical sense of the word. For that registration

1 Scot Law Com DP no 121, 2002 (available on www.scotlawcom.gov.uk). For a discussion, see articles published at 2002 SLT (News) 289 and (2002) 47 *Journal of the Law Society of Scotland* Dec/26.
2 Or perhaps even the date of execution: the law is unclear.
3 1997 SC (HL) 66.
4 1995 SC 455.

was required. But if the sellers were not divested of ownership they were at any rate divested of 'beneficial interest'; and land in which there was no beneficial interest was not part of the 'property and undertaking' of the sellers within the meaning of the legislation on floating charges.[1] Hence the land could be taken by the purchasers free from the floating charge.

Five years later the decision of the House of Lords looks less attractive than, to some eyes at least, it once did. It is true that it saves purchasers from floating charges in certain circumstances, a desirable outcome in itself. But the decision does so at the expense of insecurity of title for receivers, and of incoherence in the law of property.[2] That might not matter if *Sharp* were confined to receivers—a dying breed in any case, following the Enterprise Act 2002. But one of the uncertainties surrounding the decision was whether it might extend to other insolvency processes such as sequestration and liquidation. If so, *Sharp* is far-reaching in its effects. This was the issue considered in the important new case of *Burnett's Tr v Grainger*.[3]

Sequestration too?

Burnett's Tr was a case of sequestration. In October 1990 the Reverend Harvey and Mrs Grainger concluded missives to buy 94 Malcolm Road, Peterculter, from Mrs Burnett. The transaction settled on 8 November 1990, when the disposition was delivered in exchange for the price. The disposition was recorded in the Register of Sasines on 27 January 1992, some 14 months later. In the meantime Mrs Burnett had been sequestrated, and on 10 December 1991 her trustee completed title to the house by recording a notice of title.

Before *Sharp* the law was fairly clear: events of the kind just described would be analysed as involving what has long been known as a 'race to the register'. There would be two competitors: Mr and Mrs Grainger, and the trustee in sequestration. As usual in races, the first to get to the finishing line wins. Since it was the trustee who won the race, the property would go to him and not to the Graingers.[4] That would be painful for the Graingers, but it would be a justifiable consequence of their tardiness in registering.[5]

A wide interpretation of *Sharp*, however, would lead to a quite different analysis. Purely by delivery of the disposition Mrs Burnett would be divested of any 'beneficial interest' in the house, which would cease to form part of the 'whole estate of the debtor' within s 31(1) of the Bankruptcy (Scotland) Act 1985.

1 Insolvency Act 1986, s 53(7).

2 For a discussion, see *Conveyancing 2000* pp 94–96, and Scottish Law Commission, *Discussion Paper on Sharp v Thomson* (Scot Law Com DP no 114, 2001; available on www.scotlawcom.gov.uk) Part 2.

3 2002 SLT 699. See further S Wortley and D Reid, 'Mind the Gap: Problems in the Transfer of Ownership' (2002) 7 *Scottish Law & Practice Quarterly* 211.

4 J Burns, 'English and Scottish Bankruptcies' (1913) 29 *Law Quarterly Review* 460 at 462–464.

5 Or the tardiness of their law agents. In *Burnett's Tr v Grainger* 2002 SLT 699 at 705E Lord Coulsfield pointed out that 'in *Sharp v Thomson*, as in this case, there is every reason to think that the purchasers had a remedy against the advisers who had allowed them to place themselves or to remain in a situation in which their rights could be defeated'.

Although, therefore, the trustee had registered and the purchasers had not, the house would go to the purchasers. The trustee had reached the finishing line first, but the race would be called off.

At the first stage of the litigation in *Burnett's Tr* the sheriff principal decided that *Sharp* should be interpreted in a wide sense, and that accordingly a delivered disposition defeated the seller's sequestration.[1] An Extra Division of the Court of Session has now reversed that decision.[2] No clear *ratio*, the Division decided, could be taken from *Sharp v Thomson* itself. Lord Jauncey appeared to extend the rule in that case to all insolvency processes, but Lord Clyde—the other judge to give an opinion—was less clear and was perhaps best read as confining his opinion to floating charges alone. Furthermore, the legislation governing sequestration was different from that governing floating charges. In those circumstances the Division had a choice, and would exercise that choice in favour of the narrow view, ie the view that *Sharp* was confined to floating charges. This was partly in deference to the difficulties that had been identified since the decision in *Sharp* and partly because the coherence of property law required the rejection of beneficial interest as a right midway between personal rights and real rights. Lord Coulsfield explained matters in this way:[3]

> With the greatest respect to the views expressed by Lord Jauncey, I remain of the opinion which I expressed in *Sharp v Thomson* to the effect that the property law of Scotland should be regarded as a whole and should be given a logical and consistent application across the whole field of property, that to recognise the respondents' [the Graingers'] argument does involve a recognition of some kind of property intermediate between real and personal which is repugnant to the underlying principles of the law of Scotland and that such a recognition is liable to cause difficulty and inconsistency in the interpretation and application of the law . . . It respectfully appears to me therefore that the decision of the House of Lords should be regarded as a special decision relating only to the wording of the floating charges legislation and in particular based upon the addition of the words 'and undertaking' to the word 'property', which may involve, as Lord Clyde thought, some reference to the property available to a company for its business purposes from time to time.

This decision, which we would welcome, leaves the law in a clear and consistent state. The rules of property law as they apply on diligence and insolvency are the same as the rules that apply more generally. By those rules purchasers of heritable property are not *automatically* protected against the insolvency of the seller; but their title will be defeated if, and only if, the trustee in sequestration or liquidator completes a real right first. In practice that is most unlikely to happen unless—as in both *Sharp* and *Burnett's Tr*—there is serious delay on the part of the purchasers. The position of floating charges, however, is different. Once a disposition is delivered, the land in

1 2000 SLT (Sh Ct) 116.
2 2002 SLT 699.
3 2002 SLT 699 at 704I–J.

question is part of the 'property' but no longer of the 'undertaking' of the seller company.[1] Hence from this point on the purchaser is safe from the crystallisation of the floating charge.

Not surprisingly, the Division's decision has been appealed to the House of Lords, and it is likely to be many months before the final outcome is known. A discussion of the practical implications of *Burnett's Tr* follows, but it is necessary to bear in mind the possibility that, as with *Sharp* itself, the decision of the Court of Session is overturned in the House of Lords.

Post-delivery insolvency

Both *Sharp* and *Burnett's Tr* were concerned with post-delivery insolvency, that is, with insolvency during the period between delivery of the disposition and its registration. Almost always, this period is so short that the risk can, for all practical purposes, be discounted. Thus:

- In the case of the seller's *sequestration*, it would be virtually impossible for the trustee to complete all the stages needed for registration in the period normally taken by a purchaser to register.[2] If there is a race, therefore, there can only be one winner.
- Unlike the position for a trustee in sequestration, it is virtually unknown for *liquidators* to complete title in their own name. But even if this were to be done, under s 145 of the Insolvency Act 1986, it is inconceivable that the necessary procedure could be completed ahead of registration by a purchaser acting with normal expedition.[3] A slightly quicker procedure is available under the little-known s 25 of the Titles to Land Consolidation (Scotland) Act 1868, but even here victory to the liquidator is improbable.
- With the gradual phasing out of receivership, *administration* will become correspondingly more popular. But there is no provision for vesting of the company's property in the administrator, and hence no risk to the purchaser from post-delivery administration.
- The risk from *receivership*, although still small, is greater than in respect of other insolvency processes. This is because crystallisation of the *floating charge* occurs immediately on appointment of the receiver and without registration.[4] A floating charge also crystallises on liquidation.[5] Both cases, however, are covered by *Sharp*, so that a purchaser takes free of the floating charge.

---

1 That there might be a distinction between 'property' and 'undertaking' in this context was first suggested by Mr Scott Wortley. See G L Gretton, 'Sharp cases make good law' 1994 SLT (News) 313 at 314.
2 Scottish Law Commission, *Discussion Paper on Sharp v Thomson* (Scot Law Com DP no 114, 2001) para 4.8.
3 Scottish Law Commission, *Discussion Paper on Sharp v Thomson* para 4.24.
4 Insolvency Act 1986, ss 53 and 54.
5 Companies Act 1985, s 463(1).

Pre-delivery insolvency

If the seller is already insolvent *before* delivery, this fact will usually be in the public domain and so known to the purchaser by means of searches in the appropriate registers—the Register of Inhibitions and Adjudication, the Companies Register, and the Register of Insolvencies. However, searches, and the Registers themselves, are slightly out of date, so that an insolvency shortly before settlement might go undetected. In that case any disposition granted by the seller—or, in the case of a company, by the directors—would be void as lacking in capacity.[1] In practice, the risk is slight. The only reported case of pre-delivery insolvency is *Gibson v Hunter Home Designs Ltd*,[2] a case in which, contrary to normal practice, the price was paid without delivery of the disposition. But in any event the risk is generally covered by the letter of obligation or, in the case of floating charges, by the lender's certificate of non-crystallisation. In its recent *Discussion Paper on Sharp v Thomson*, the Scottish Law Commission makes a number of proposals designed to provide additional protection in this situation.[3] It is important to notice that, even on the wider reading rejected by the Extra Division in *Burnett's Tr*, no protection is offered by *Sharp* against insolvency prior to delivery of the disposition.

Trust clause

After the decision at first instance in *Sharp* it became fashionable to use a trust clause in the disposition, ie a clause by which the seller holds the land in trust for the purchaser pending registration.[4] Some nine years later, the fashion has lost some of its allure but not all of its exponents. Trust clauses have been attacked, and also defended, on grounds both of workability and of desirability.[5] Whatever the merits of that debate, however, it may be doubted whether trust clauses now serve any useful purpose. Insofar as they offer protection at all, they protect only against post-delivery insolvency. But here protection is already afforded in relation to floating charges by the decision in *Sharp*, and in the case of other insolvency processes the risk seems too small to justify the step of establishing a trust. After all, trusts have consequences. Some of the consequences are complex. Not all the consequences may be welcome to the parties.

Sale by receivers

One type of transaction deserves special mention. Following *Sharp*, it can no longer be taken for granted that a receiver has title to all of the company's land as disclosed by the register. For at the time of crystallisation there may have been one or more dispositions by the company which had been delivered but

---

1 Scottish Law Commission, *Discussion Paper on Sharp v Thomson* para 3.4.
2 1976 SC 23.
3 Scot Law Com DP no 114, 2001 Part 4.
4 The idea was first suggested by Robert Rennie, 'Dead on Delivery' 1994 SLT (News) 183.
5 A J M Steven and S Wortley, 'The Perils of a Trusting Disposition' 1996 SLT (News) 365; J Chalmers, 'In Defence of the Trusting Conveyancer' 2002 SLT (News) 231.

not yet registered. In that event the land carried by such a disposition would escape the floating charge and could not be dealt with by the receiver. Such deeds, no doubt, will be both rare and, in most cases, promptly registered, so that within a month or so of receivership the position will be clear. But the risk remains of a latent disposition which is unknown both to the receiver and to any person acquiring from the receiver. One effect of *Sharp*, therefore, is to cast doubt on the title offered by receivers—an inevitable consequence of the decision to allow an unregistered event (delivery of the disposition) to have legal effect against third parties.

So far, the approach of the Keeper has been to accept titles granted by receivers without exclusion of indemnity. The relevant passage in the *Registration of Title Practice Book*[1] is worth quoting in full:

> The Keeper considers that the risk of a latent unregistered disposition surfacing once registration has been completed is too small to justify a policy of blanket indemnity exclusion for all sales by receivers. Accordingly, an application for registration of a conveyance by a receiver will not result in an exclusion of indemnity solely because of the risk that an unregistered disposition may come to light. Nevertheless the Keeper expects that a purchaser acting in good faith will make appropriate enquiries of the receiver. If the receiver's response to those enquiries is less than satisfactory, or points to some difficulty or anomaly, the purchaser should seek the advice of the Keeper's Pre-Registration Enquiries Section before proceeding to settle the transaction. Pre-Registration Enquiries will take a measured view of the circumstances and consider the risk to the Keeper's position.

Whether this approach would survive a major claim on the indemnity fund remains a matter for the future.

JUDICIAL RECTIFICATION

Take the following example. Mrs Smith buys a house. It is subject to a deed of conditions registered some ten years ago. Her law agent looks over the deed and is satisfied by its contents. The transaction is settled and she moves in. Six months later the original developers apply to court to have the deed of conditions rectified under s 8 of the Law Reform (Miscellaneous Provisions) (Scotland) Act 1985. Perhaps some of the intended terms were missed out by mistake; or perhaps a condition needs to be re-expressed if it is to be legally effective.[2] Assuming that rectification is granted, its effect is, generally, retrospective. In other words, following registration of the decree[3] the deed of conditions is taken always to have been in its rectified form.[4] Sometimes a change carried out in this way

1 Paragraph 5.37.

2 See *Bank of Ireland v Bass Brewers Ltd* 2000 GWD 20-786 and 2000 GWD 28-1077, discussed in *Conveyancing 2000* pp 118–119.

3 Or, in the case of the Land Register, rectification of the Register, generally under s 9(3)(b) of the Land Registration (Scotland) Act 1979.

4 Land Registration (Scotland) Act 1979, s 9(3A); Law Reform (Miscellaneous Provisions) (Scotland) Act 1985, s 8(5).

might not matter very much. It might be innocuous, or merely technical, or at any rate have no impact on the use of the property. But sometimes that would not be so. Perhaps Mrs Smith runs a business from home. If so, the importation of a prohibition against business use would threaten her livelihood. What then can be done? The answer is that the 1985 Act gives protection of two different kinds. In the first place, s 9 contains provisions designed to protect third parties who relied on the deed in its unrectified form. And in the second place, under s 8(1) the court has an overriding discretion to grant, or to refuse, rectification. Both were invoked in *Sheltered Housing Management Ltd v Cairns*.[1]

The litigation concerned a sheltered housing complex in Falkirk, originally constructed by Barratt (Falkirk) Ltd but now managed by Sheltered Housing Management Ltd (SHML), who had also acquired the superiority. The proof disclosed considerable unrest within the development. Residents had divided into two camps. A minority was in a state of what Lord Nimmo Smith described as 'organised resistance'.[2] These owners objected to the management methods adopted by SHML and in particular to the lack of consultation and accountability. As a result they had ceased to pay the service charge. The remaining owners, apparently, were content with matters and paid the service charge when due.[3] Relations between the two groups were not good. 'The non-payers', observed Lord Nimmo Smith, 'do not go on social outings with the payers.'[4] Since it was impractical to supply services—such as a warden, or insurance—to some owners but not to others, SHML continued to provide a management service and, in the case of the non-payers, met the cost themselves.

It might be thought that SHML would simply sue for the unpaid service charge. But there was a difficulty. When the deed of conditions was engrossed for execution the clause requiring payment of the service charge was left out. This meant that, while SHML had an obligation to supply services, they had no corresponding right to collect the service charge. For a long time no one noticed, but eventually this became the legal basis of the non-payers' resistance.

In this litigation SHML sought rectification of the deed of conditions to the effect of adding the payment clause which had been omitted by mistake.[5] Inevitably, some non-payers were successors who had bought, not from Barratt, but from an intermediate owner. Rectification, they argued, would be to their prejudice and was not within the power of the court.

The argument turned mainly on s 9 of the 1985 Act. In order for a third party, such as the non-payers, to benefit from the s 9 protection, three conditions must

1 2002 Hous LR 126.

2 Paragraph 11. It seems that this extended to other complexes under the same management and had led to the formation of an association known as the Sheltered Housing Owners' Confederation (SHOC). The Title Conditions (Scotland) Bill makes a number of changes to the operation of sheltered housing, with the aim of improving accountability.

3 At any given time, however, up to 10 of the 53 units were owned by SHML and occupied by tenants. See para 18.

4 Paragraph 19.

5 The application was made under s 8(1)(a) of the 1985 Act because, unusually with deeds of conditions, the deed could be presented as having been drawn up in implement of a prior agreement with SHML. The draft deed annexed to the agreement included the missing clause.

be satisfied: (1) the third party must have changed his or her position in a material way ('acted or refrained from acting') in reliance on the document in its unrectified form; (2) the third party must have been in good faith, or at any rate the reliance must have been reasonable; and (3) rectification must be materially prejudicial to the third party. Usually the third condition will be satisfied without difficulty, so that the real issue concerns conditions (1) and (2).

In *Sheltered Housing Management Ltd* attention focused on condition (1). It appeared that at the time of purchase the non-payers had not known that the payment clause was missing. Indeed at first they had paid the service charge, as if the clause was not omitted after all. But specific knowledge, Lord Nimmo Smith held, was crucial:[1]

> I do not see how somebody could be said to have relied on the terms of the document if all he knew was that the document existed and did not know what its terms were. His position could not be said to have been affected to a material extent unless he knew about, and relied upon, the terms in respect of which rectification is sought.

Hence the non-payers fell at the first hurdle. Lord Nimmo Smith's remarks must, of course, be taken in the context in which they were made. It would be unrealistic to expect of a purchaser detailed knowledge of a deed of conditions (although a solicitor would normally have examined the deed on his or her behalf). And if a purchaser does not know all the clauses that are present in a deed, he or she cannot be expected to be able to list the, potentially infinite, number of clauses which are not present and on whose absence there is supposedly reliance.

Given the non-payers' state of knowledge, it was unnecessary for the court to consider the more difficult aspect of condition (1). This is whether the omitted clause was sufficiently material to have resulted in the change of position. In practice an unrectified clause is likely to be only one of a number of factors leading to the decision to act (or to refrain from acting). Usually it would be difficult to say that it was the sole—or even the main—determinative factor. Few people, after all, buy (or decline to buy) a house on the basis of the conditions in the title. A too literal interpretation of condition (1), therefore, may make s 9 unworkable.

Condition (2) was not discussed by the court, but there too the non-payers might have been in difficulties. For a deed of conditions which imposes a duty on the managers to supply services without imposing a corresponding duty on the owners to meet the cost is, one might have thought, an object of suspicion which would prompt further inquiry.[2] This was the argument advanced, in comparable circumstances, in another case from 2002, *Co-operative Wholesale Society Ltd v Ravenseft Properties Ltd*.[3] The main issue was whether the same

1 Paragraph 14.

2 See Scottish Law Commission, *Report on Rectification of Contractual and Other Documents* (Scot Law Com no 79, 1983) para 6.7, commenting that the condition 'would not . . . impose an unrealistic burden upon a third party to discover what lay behind the written terms of a document, but, on the other hand, it would not absolve him from turning a blind eye to facts which should at least have raised doubt in his mind'.

3 2002 SCLR 644. An earlier stage in the same litigation was noted at 2001 GWD 24-905 (*Conveyancing 2001* Case (80) and p 121).

factual basis—namely the apparent oddity of the deed—could be used for both alternatives allowed by condition (2) (ie bad faith or unreasonable reliance). In Lord Macfadyen's view it could:[1]

> There are, no doubt, many ways in which a person may come within the scope of section 9(3)(b) [unreasonable reliance]. I am, however, satisfied that the pursuers are correct in their submission that one way in which a person may do so is if circumstances which fall short of bringing home to him actual or imputed knowledge of the mistake in expression in the document [ie bad faith] nevertheless raise a sufficient doubt as to whether it is correctly expressed to make it unreasonable to rely on it without further inquiry. If such is the case, a person who makes no inquiry may be held to have acted unreasonably in relying on the document.

Rectification is a power rather than a duty. In terms of s 8(1) a court can choose not to rectify even where the conditions for rectification have been met, although that would be unusual in practice.[2] Some consideration was given to this issue in *Sheltered Housing Management Ltd*. Lord Nimmo Smith pointed to the community of interest of the residents in a sheltered housing development, and to the disruption caused by the dispute between payers and non-payers. Only the restoration of the omitted clause provided a way out of the impasse. Hence it was appropriate to exercise the power to rectify.

ADULTS WITH INCAPACITY (SCOTLAND) ACT 2000[3]

Introduction

Part 6 of the Adults with Incapacity (Scotland) Act 2000 came into force on 1 April 2002. It provides a new legislative regime for dealing with the affairs of adults with mental health problems. Many solicitors will be affected by the provisions, especially as there is an ever-increasing elderly population in Scotland.[4] It is no longer competent to appoint a *curator bonis*.[5] Instead the 2000 Act introduces two new types of appointee whom a court can empower to act on behalf of an adult who lacks legal capacity. First, there are authorised persons (also known as 'intervenors') who are given power to act in relation to a specific matter.[6] Their authority to act is limited in terms of the intervention

1 2002 SCLR 644 at 652D. Proof before answer was allowed.
2 G L Gretton and K G C Reid, *Conveyancing* (2nd edn, 1999) para 17.07.
3 This part is contributed by Andrew J M Steven and Alan Barr, both of the University of Edinburgh. The authors are grateful to Alistair Rennie and John Glover of Registers of Scotland, Stuart Fowler of the Office of the Public Guardian, and Sheriff Nigel Morrison QC for their assistance. While the text has been prepared with care, no responsibility is accepted by the authors or the University of Edinburgh for actions taken or omissions deriving from the material herein.
4 The Justice Minister, Mr Jim Wallace MSP, advised the Scottish Parliament during the passage of the legislation that around 100,000 people in Scotland are affected by incapacity at any one time: see *Official Report*, 9 December 1999, col 1376.
5 Adults with Incapacity (Scotland) Act 2000, s 80.
6 2000 Act, s 53.

order made in their favour by the sheriff. Secondly, there are guardians, who are similar to *curators bonis* in that they are given wide-ranging powers to act in relation to all or most matters on behalf of the adult.[1] Both authorised persons and guardians act under the supervision of the Office of the Public Guardian, which is based in Falkirk.[2]

The 2000 Act contains special procedures which must be followed when a conveyancing transaction involves an adult with incapacity. There exists an extremely helpful *Briefing Note* on these by Mr Ian Davis, the Director of Legal Services at the Registers of Scotland.[3] Given that the Act is new, practice in relation to it by the Keeper, the Public Guardian and the legal profession will take some time to develop, so to an extent this commentary is provisional.

The key provisions of the 2000 Act affecting conveyancers are s 56, which deals with the registration of an intervention order relating to heritable property, and s 61, which is its equivalent provision in relation to guardianship orders. The idea behind ss 56 and 61 is that the transfer of a right of management to an authorised person or a guardian, will only affect third parties if the sheriff's interlocutor is registered. Curiously, this example of the publicity principle does not extend to attorneys acting under continuing powers of attorney.[4] More generally, it is not apparent why registration is required for representatives of an individual who happen to be guardians or authorised persons under the Act, whereas it is excused for representatives who are not.[5]

Obtaining power to deal with heritable property

The need to register

A brief treatment of some aspects of the court procedures involved in appointing either a guardian or an authorised person is given later.[6] But for present purposes it is convenient to start from the moment that the sheriff grants an interlocutor giving an authorised person or guardian the power to deal with heritable property. Sections 56(3) (authorised persons) and 61(3) (guardians) provide that application be made by that person 'forthwith' to the Keeper for recording of the interlocutor containing the order in the Register of Sasines or for registering it in the Land Register. The only significant difference between the provisions is that if a guardian has been ordered to find caution, this must be done before applying to the Keeper.

1 2000 Act, s 57. Note that the term 'incapax' is no longer used under the new legislation. The replacement term is simply 'adult'.
2 Its website is at www.publicguardian-scotland.gov.uk.
3 See www.ros.gov.uk/press_releases/awi_pr_29_04_02.pdf.
4 See Part 2 of the 2000 Act, which came into force on 2 April 2001. For commentary, see Alan Barr, 'Drafting Powers of Attorney under the New Regime', The Edinburgh Law Review Seminar Series, 2001.
5 For example, an individual acting under a standard power of attorney.
6 See pp 108–110. See further Alan Barr and David Nichols, 'Intervention and Guardianship for Adults with Incapacity', The Edinburgh Law Review Seminar Series, 2002.

The provisions place a positive duty to register as soon as possible. However, no actual penalty is imposed for late registration. Further, the provisions do not actually state that an order is not valid until registered. This may be contrasted with continuing and welfare powers of attorney under the 2000 Act which are provided to be inoperative until registration with the Public Guardian.[1]

The Keeper has specific requirements as regards the submission of the interlocutor.[2] Where the intervention or guardianship order is an extract decree, he will be prepared to accept the original of this, because an extract decree is authenticated by the court.[3] Where, however, the order is not in the form of a extract decree, he will require a copy which has been certified as true by a solicitor, a clerk of the court, or a member of the Public Guardian's staff.

Interlocutor cannot be a midcouple

As the interlocutor must be registered forthwith, the Keeper is not prepared to accept it as a midcouple.[4] It will therefore not be possible to deduce title through an interlocutor.

Identification of the property

The interlocutor must specify the affected property in a way that makes it identifiable in either the Register of Sasines or the Land Register.[5] Whilst the pronouncement of the interlocutor is, of course, a matter for the sheriff, the sheriff will be unable to fulfil this requirement unless the person making the application has provided the necessary information. As regards Land Register property, s 15(1) of the Land Registration (Scotland) Act 1979 applies, requiring a reference to the title number. As regards the Register of Sasines, the Keeper will require either a particular description or a description by reference to a recorded deed. In either case, the description must 'give the public adequate notice of the subjects involved'.[6] In practice, however, it seems that the Keeper will apply the same rules as for standard securities. Those rules were recently relaxed by the Abolition of Feudal Tenure etc (Scotland) Act 2000, so that the property need only be described in a manner sufficient to identify it.[7]

Registrable and non-registrable orders

Intervention or guardianship orders require to be registered only where they give the power 'to deal with, convey or manage any interest in land' which is registered or capable of being registered in the Register of Sasines or the Land Register.[8] The Keeper's basic rule is that an order should be registered if it gives power to enter into an

1 2000 Act, s 19(1). However, as noted already, registration in the Register of Sasines or Land Register is not required.
2 *Briefing Note* para 2.6.
3 The Keeper will require that a copy extract decree is certified as a true copy.
4 *Briefing Note* para 2.2.
5 2000 Act, ss 56(1), 61(2).
6 *Briefing Note* para 2.5.
7 *Conveyancing 2000* pp 141–143.
8 2000 Act, ss 56(1), 61(1).

activity in which a search or equivalent report might be obtained. In the Keeper's interpretation the requirement is for interlocutors empowering dealings, conveyances or management activities of authorised persons or guardians which alter the real or quasi-real heritable rights of the adult.

The words 'which are capable of registration' should perhaps be added to the last sentence. The purist might also ask what a 'quasi-real heritable right' is.

The *Briefing Note* gives examples of orders which, in the Keeper's view, should or should not be registered.[1] In the former category are orders granting powers to acquire or dispose of land, to grant, assign or renounce long leases, and to grant or vary heritable securities. The power to discharge a heritable security would also necessitate registration. The principal example in the latter category is an order giving powers in relation to short leases. Another example might be the right to renounce occupancy rights under the Matrimonial Homes Act. If there is doubt about whether registration is required under the 2000 Act, the Keeper suggests that his Pre-Registration Enquiries Section be contacted.

Registering the interlocutor

Where an interlocutor is registrable, ss 56(4) and 61(4) require that an application must be made to the Keeper for its registration. The application must contain:

(1) the name and address of the authorised person or guardian;

(2) a statement that the authorised person or guardian has powers relating to each property specified in the order; and

(3) a copy of the interlocutor.

There is helpful advice in the *Briefing Note*[2] about how to satisfy these requirements, together with appropriate checklists as to what must be submitted depending on which type of interlocutor or which Register is involved. In a Sasines Register case, application should be made using the CPB2 Form. In a Land Register case, Form 2 should be used. In both cases, the application attracts the miscellaneous event fee, currently £25.

The end result in the Register of Sasines is that the interlocutor will be placed on the computerised Register, the Keeper will affix the Register's stamp and seal to the actual document, and return it to the presenting agent.[3] In the Land Register, the interlocutor will be noted in the B section of the title sheet.[4] The authorised person or guardian is then required to send the stamped and sealed interlocutor (in a Sasine case) or the updated land certificate, or a copy thereof, to the Public Guardian, who will enter the details into his own Register maintained in terms of s 6(2)(b) of the 2000 Act.[5]

1 Paragraphs 3.2–3.3.
2 Paragraphs 4.1–4.4.
3 2000 Act, ss 56(5), 61(5).
4 2000 Act, ss 56(6), 56(7).
5 2000 Act, ss 56(7), 61(7).

Sale of land

Obtaining the power to sell

An authorised person or guardian who wishes to sell land owned by the adult on whose behalf he acts must first obtain the necessary power from the sheriff and have the interlocutor registered, as discussed above. At the very latest, the interlocutor must be registered contemporaneously with the disposition.[1] Where a guardian is selling accommodation used by the adult as a dwelling house, the consent of the Public Guardian is needed, and in practice must be obtained before the property is marketed.[2] In Land Register cases the Keeper will wish to see the consent before issuing a land certificate without exclusion of indemnity.

Where an authorised person is selling and an obligation to find caution has been imposed in terms of s 53(7) of the 2000 Act, this obligation will also have to be fulfilled in advance of the sale and exhibited to the Keeper. In the case of a guardian, the Keeper will already have examined evidence of caution if the interlocutor was registered in the Land Register. If, however, the order was registered in the Register of Sasines, evidence of caution will be needed for the first registration induced by the sale.[3]

Missives

No alteration seems required to the standard offer to purchase, because production of the requisite documentation in terms of the 2000 Act will be covered by the general obligation to give a good and marketable title.[4] On the other hand, it is important for the selling solicitors to state in the missives that they are acting in terms of the instructions of an authorised person or guardian. This ensures that the authorised person or guardian is liable on the missives only in that capacity. Otherwise the authorised person or guardian will be personally liable, although they may be reimbursed out of the adult's estate in respect of any successful claim made against them, provided that they have complied with their obligations under the rest of the 2000 Act.[5]

In the case of sales of accommodation used by the adult as a dwelling house, the consent of the Public Guardian will be required as to the price.[6] This means that a suspensive condition may have to be placed in the qualified acceptance stating that the sale is dependent on that consent. Much depends on how quickly the Public Guardian is able to process the application for consent. As part of that application, he will need certain information, in particular the price which is to be accepted, all offers which were received, and a valuation of the property.[7]

---

1 See *Briefing Note* paras 5.3–5.4.

2 2000 Act, Sch 2, para 6(1).

3 *Briefing Note* para 5.5.

4 In the same way that the duty of a selling heritable creditor to comply with the Mortgage Rights (Scotland) Act 2001 is encompassed in the duty to provide a good and marketable title: see *Conveyancing 2001* pp 84–85.

5 2000 Act, s 67(4) (guardians). The provision is applied to authorised persons by s 53(14).

6 2000 Act, s 53(6), Sch 2, para 6(1).

7 In this regard, the Scottish Court Service and the Office of the Public Guardian have produced guidance notes and an application form.

A fee of £100 is payable. It is understood that the Public Guardian hopes to process applications within three days and in some cases his turnaround time may be as little as 24 hours.[1] However, if the process proves lengthier, a suspensive condition may be the only option.

Letter of obligation

For the purposes of the sale the instructing client is, strictly, the adult with incapacity. The authorised person or guardian is his or her representative. The adult should therefore be placed in the heading of the letter of obligation as the selling client. It is easy to get confused by the fact that the authorised person or guardian may also be a client in his or her own right. For example, a guardian who is given advice as regards rights and duties can be regarded as a client at least to that extent. However, for present purposes, the adult is the client.

Disposition

There follows a style disposition, which is developed from the style suggested in the *Briefing Note*.[2] The disponer here is an authorised person, but the style can easily be altered for guardians.

> I, GORDON BENNETT,[A] residing at Fifty South Bridge, Glasgow, being an authorised person under an intervention order in terms of section 53 of the Adults with Incapacity (Scotland) Act 2000 conform to interlocutor issued by the Sheriff of Glasgow and Strathkelvin on Twenty Eighth February Two Thousand and Three[B] in respect of the affairs of SAFFRON TAYLOR, residing formerly at The Grange, Atlantic Road, Glasgow, and now at the River City Nursing Home, Clyde Street, Glasgow,[C] the heritable proprietor of the subjects and others hereinafter disponed, in consideration of the price of FIFTY THOUSAND POUNDS (£50,000) paid to me by BERNIE THE BUILDER LIMITED, a Company incorporated under the Companies Acts (Company Number SC 12345) and having its Registered Office at Seventeen York Street, Cumbernauld, hereby DISPONE to and in favour of the said Bernie the Builder Limited ALL and WHOLE that plot of ground lying to the north of Atlantic Road, Glasgow in the County of the Burgh and Regality of Glasgow and extending to twelve decimal or one hundredth parts of a hectare (0.12 ha) or thereby all as the said plot is hatched and outlined in red on the plan annexed and subscribed as relative hereto, being part of the subjects registered under Title Number GLA 54321; BUT RESERVING IN FAVOUR of the said Saffron Taylor and her heirs and successors[D] as proprietors of the subjects registered under the aforementioned title number under exception of the subjects hereby disponed a pedestrian servitude right of way over the footpath delineated in blue on the said plan; WITH ENTRY and actual occupation on Tenth April Two Thousand and Three; And I grant warrandice from my facts and deeds only and bind the said Saffron Taylor in absolute warrandice[E]; and I as authorised person foresaid[F] certify that the transaction hereby effected does not form part of a larger transaction or of a series of transactions in respect of which the amount

1 The Explanatory Notes to the 2000 Act, para 425, recognise the essence of speed here, stating that applications to the Public Guardian 'will generally need to be done very quickly because of the Scottish legal system'.

2 Paragraph 5.1.

or value or the aggregate amount or value of the consideration exceeds sixty thousand pounds: IN WITNESS WHEREOF

Notes

A The Keeper's suggested style followed here runs the deed in the name of the authorised person, which may seem rather curious given that the adult remains the owner. It is accepted practice that deeds granted by an attorney may run in the name of the attorney as well as in the name of the principal[1] and presumably the Keeper is applying that principle here.

B The Keeper's suggested style does not refer to the relevant interlocutor. Whilst this interlocutor will require to be on the Register, or registered contemporaneously with the disposition, to enable the authorised person to dispone in terms of the Act, it is felt that the deed is given increased clarity by referring to it.

C There is a strong possibility that the adult will have moved address, particularly if it is the home which is being sold.

D Where rights are being reserved—for example, servitude rights, the right to enforce real burdens or ownership of minerals—these should be reserved to the adult, who remains the owner, rather than the authorised person or guardian.

E It is suggested that the appropriate type of warrandice is fact and deed warrandice, as with trustees and executors. However, the adult (not the adult's estate as this is not vested in the authorised person or guardian) should be bound in absolute warrandice.[2]

F The stamp clause should be certified by the authorised person or guardian in that capacity.

Personal search

When purchasing property owned by an adult with incapacity, it is necessary to search against the adult in the Personal Register. It is not necessary to search against the guardian or authorised person, on the basis that the right of that person, being non-transferable, is not adjudgeable and therefore not subject to diligence.[3] It would furthermore not be possible for a guardian or authorised person to be sequestrated in that capacity because no property is held in that capacity.

Matrimonial Homes (Family Protection) (Scotland) Act 1981

The Keeper's policy in relation to sales by *curators bonis* will be applied to sales by guardians and authorised persons.[4] The Keeper's view is that such a sale is not a dealing by the adult and no Matrimonial Homes Act evidence is needed. There is, however, some doubt as to whether the Keeper is correct on this point,

1 G L Gretton and K G C Reid, *Conveyancing* (2nd edn, 1999) para 14.14.
2 This is how warrandice is granted in dispositions by factors and commissioners, and by parents on behalf of children: see *Encyclopaedia of Scottish Legal Styles* vol 4 pp 219 and 251.
3 G L Gretton, *The Law of Inhibition and Adjudication* (2nd edn, 1996) pp 215–216.
4 *Briefing Note* para 5.2. See *Registration of Title Practice Book* para 6.41.

and the safest approach is to obtain appropriate documentation.[1] This means a consent from the spouse if there is one. If the adult is not married, a non-statutory affidavit can be obtained from the guardian, or authorised person, or another person who has knowledge of the adult's circumstances, to the effect that he believes to the best of his knowledge that the adult is single. Some may question, however, whether it is really necessary to insist on documentation if the Keeper does not want to see it. If the Keeper is prepared to add a note in the title sheet stating that there are no subsisting occupancy rights, and a non-entitled spouse of an adult with incapacity later successfully claims occupancy rights, then indemnity will in principle be payable to the new proprietor.[2]

Settlement

Given below is a checklist as to the special matters which a conveyancer purchasing land from a guardian or authorised person must check before being prepared to settle the transaction. It is based on paragraphs 5.3–5.5 of the *Briefing Note*. The conveyancer acting for a purchaser from a guardian or authorised person must ensure that:

(1) the transaction is within the powers conferred by the intervention or guardianship order;

(2) the intervention or guardianship interlocutor has been registered or recorded in advance, or that a contemporaneous registration application is being made;

(3) the disposition is drafted in the form approved by the Keeper;

(4) the letter of obligation is in the appropriate form;

(5) evidence is supplied that caution has been obtained if the sheriff has required this in terms of s 53(7) (authorised persons) or s 58(6) (guardians, first registration only) of the 2000 Act;

(6) where the subjects are used as a dwellinghouse by the adult, the Public Guardian has given consent as to the consideration received, in terms of s 53(6) (authorised persons), or his consent both to the sale in principle and to the consideration received in terms of Sch 2, para 6(1) (guardians) of the 2000 Act; and

(7) Matrimonial Homes Act consent/renunciation or non-statutory affidavit is available.

On (1), it is understood that if the transaction is not within the powers of the authorised person or guardian, the Keeper will simply reject the application for registration.[3] The 2000 Act does, however, provide that where a third party acquires, in good faith and for value, title to any interest in heritable property from an authorised person or guardian, the title is not challengeable only because the authorised person or guardian acted outwith the scope of his authority.[4] It is

1 See G L Gretton and K G C Reid, *Conveyancing* (2nd edn, 1999) para 10.21.

2 *Registration of Title Practice Book* para 6.29.

3 His view is that it is vexatious to attempt to dispone someone else's property without the requisite authority and therefore that the Land Registration (Scotland) Act 1979, s 4(2)(c) applies.

4 2000 Act, ss 53(13), 79(b). Indemnity is not payable by the Keeper to a person who suffers a loss as a result of these provisions: see the 1979 Act, s 12(3)(kk) (added by the 2000 Act Sch 5, para 14).

difficult to see how these provisions will come into play, given the Keeper's policy. In any event, it is questionable whether a person who transacts with an authorised person or guardian and does not trouble to check the powers, particularly given that the order conferring these powers requires to be registered, can be said to be in good faith.

Of greater practical importance is the equivalent rule protecting against irregularity of procedure in the making of the intervention order or guardianship order,[1] for third parties cannot be expected to check the court process in relation to the appointment. Equally important is s 77(4) of the 2000 Act, which protects against termination of authority prior to the actual creation or transfer of the title.[2] This would apply if, for example, the Public Guardian recalls the powers of a guardian,[3] but the transaction proceeds without the purchaser being aware of this.

On (2), if the interlocutor is not already registered and a contemporaneous registration application is not made, the Keeper will adopt the steps which are set out at paragraph 5.4 of the *Briefing Note*. In the first place, he will contact the presenting agent and suggest that the application for registration is withdrawn until an application for registration of the empowering interlocutor is made. If the presenting agent refuses, the Keeper will make a requisition requiring the interlocutor within 60 days. If this requisition is not satisfied, the application for registration of the disposition will be rejected. If it is satisfied, the Keeper will exclude indemnity in respect of any problem arising out of the disponee's interest pre-dating that of the authorised person or guardian.

On (3), if the disposition is not in the correct form, the Keeper will reject the application. It is therefore important to comply with his suggested style.

On (5), if evidence of caution is not presented, the Keeper will contact the presenting agent. If evidence is still not forthcoming, the Keeper's likely course of action will not be to reject the application outright, but to exclude indemnity.

On (6), the Keeper's approach will be similar as to (5).

On (7), as discussed above, some conveyancers may take the view that such documentation is not required, given the policy of the Keeper.

Purchase of land

Obtaining authority and consent

The position is perhaps less straightforward where land is being acquired for an adult with incapacity. The authorised person or guardian, needing, it seems, authority from the sheriff for the purchase,[4] will wish to have the authorising interlocutor duly registered before proceeding, to avoid personal liability on the transaction. But there is a difficulty. In terms of ss 56(2) and 61(2) of the 2000

1 2000 Act, ss 53(13), 79(a). Again, no indemnity is payable by the Keeper in terms of s 12(3)(kk) of the 1979 Act.
2 Once more, no indemnity is payable by the Keeper in terms of s 12(3)(kk) of the 1979 Act.
3 2000 Act, s 73(1). This might be done if the adult regains capacity.
4 2000 Act, ss 56(1), 61(1), discussed below.

Act the sheriff's interlocutor must specify the property in a way in which it can be identified in the registers. Yet at this stage what it is to be bought is unlikely to be known. The result is a vicious circle. The application cannot be made without specifying the property, but the property cannot be bid for without successfully making the application.

This problem may be because ss 56 and 61 were not designed to deal with the situation where the adult is acquiring property. Rather, they seem aimed at property already owned by the adult at the time when the authorised person or guardian is appointed. Thus the provisions apply to orders vesting in the authorised person or guardian 'any right [of the adult] to deal with, convey or manage any interest in heritable property';[1] and it is easy to argue that an adult has a right to 'deal with, convey or manage' property only if he already owns it.[2] The Keeper's view, however, is that the provisions extend to acquisitions.[3] A further point is that the acquisition may be funded and therefore involve the granting of a standard security. If so, the provisions clearly apply to such a grant. Accordingly, a way has to be found to deal with them.

The suggested solution is a two-stage court process. Stage 1 would be an application to purchase in general terms. An interim interlocutor could be granted by the sheriff. This would be done in advance of bidding for the property. There are then two possibilities as regards stage 2.

One is to intimate the actual purchase by motion. The sheriff would then grant a further interlocutor if content to do so, and this would be capable of registration. Provided that the Public Guardian had consented to the purchase, it is unlikely that a sheriff would refuse to grant the second interlocutor. This would particularly be the case if as much detail as possible were placed in the original application, including a request to agree to a specific price range and locality. The use of a motion would not, however, be without difficulty. It is unclear whether an appearance would be necessary and what, if any, intimation requirements would apply.[4]

---

1 The words in the square brackets are only found in s 61(1) and not in s 56(1) of the 2000 Act.

2 This argument is given some weight by the original wording of the provision relating to guardians when the Act was first introduced as a Bill into the Scottish Parliament. It stated (s 55(1)): 'This section applies where the sheriff makes a guardianship order which confers powers relating to heritable property of the adult.' The provision was recast in its current form at Stage 2 to make it clear 'that only guardianship orders that can confer powers that are relevant to the title to an adult's property need be registered in the Land Register or General Register of Sasines' (Mr Angus Mackay MSP, Deputy Minister for Justice, *Official Report, Justice and Home Affairs Committee*, 1 Feb 2000, col 718). Again, the Minister's words suggest present rather than future property.

3 See *Briefing Note* para 2.3.

4 The intimation requirements of an originating application for intervention or guardianship are extensive: see Act of Sederunt (Summary Applications, Statutory Applications and Appeals etc Rules) 1999 (SI 1999/929), r 3.16.4 (as added by the Act of Sederunt (Summary Applications, Statutory Applications and Appeals etc Rules) Amendment (Adults with Incapacity) 2001 (SSI 2001/142) and amended by the Act of Sederunt (Summary Applications, Statutory Applications and Appeals etc Rules) Amendment (No 3) (Adults with Incapacity) 2002 (SSI 2002/146)).

The second possibility is that the sheriff, in the initial interlocutor, could delegate the power to the sheriff clerk to add the description of the property to that same interlocutor when it had been identified and purchased. This would seem to be the preferable option, as it means that a motion is not required. Whether sheriffs will be prepared to adopt such a practice remains to be seen.

If the property is to be used as accommodation for the adult with incapacity, the consent of the Public Guardian is also needed, both as to the price and, in the case of guardians only, to the principle as well.[1] Consent to the principle can be given well in advance, but whether consent to the price can be obtained in the interval between survey and making the offer is less clear and may vary from case to case. The Public Guardian will need to be given a considerable amount of information, including the address, price, sales particulars and a copy of the survey report. As with consent to sales, discussed earlier, the Public Guardian hopes to process applications within three days and in some cases his turnaround time may be as little as 24 hours. A fee of £100 is payable. If the Public Guardian has not made a ruling before the closing date, a suspensive condition will be needed in the offer. The practical problem here is that if the highest offer is made on behalf of an adult with incapacity, but the second highest offer is only a few hundred pounds short and has no suspensive conditions, the seller may simply opt for the lower offer. The desirability of getting the relevant paperwork to the Public Guardian as far as possible in advance of the closing date is self-evident.

The problems just described are for the buyer and not for the seller. There is no need for the seller's solicitor to check that the requirements of the 2000 Act are met, because if the authorised person or guardian does not have authority to act, then he or she will be personally liable upon the transaction. In particular, he or she will be personally liable to pay the price.[2]

Disposition

The disposition should convey the property to the adult with incapacity, not to the authorised person or guardian.[3] The deed may, however, narrate that the authorised person or guardian paid the price.

Letter of obligation

The letter of obligation should refer to the adult with incapacity, as the person who is to become owner. Therefore, as with sales on behalf of an adult with incapacity, the adult's name requires to be inserted as a client in the heading of the letter.

Settlement

In relation to a Land Register transaction, the Keeper will require:[4]

---

1 2000 Act, s 53(6), Sch 2, para 6(1).
2 Although, as noted earlier, ss 67(4) and 53(14) of the 2000 Act may give some relief.
3 *Briefing Note* para 6.
4 *Briefing Note* para 6.

(1) evidence that the authorised person or guardian has power to purchase;
(2) that the interlocutor conferring that power is registered contemporaneously with the disposition;[1]
(3) that the disposition is in the correct form;
(4) evidence that any requirement to find caution has been met; and
(5) evidence that any necessary consents from the Public Guardian have been obtained.

Failure to comply with these requirements will produce results similar to those described above in relation to the sale by a guardian or authorised person.[2]

Discharging standard securities

Discharges are the subject of specific guidance in the *Briefing Note*.[3] Where, as usually, the adult with incapacity is the *debtor*—and hence the grantee—no change is needed to the style at Form F in the Conveyancing and Feudal Reform (Scotland) Act 1970, Schedule 4. If the loan was repaid, either partly or in full, by the authorised person or guardian, then this may be narrated in the deed. The Keeper will not require evidence of the authorised person or guardian's power to act.

Where the adult is the *creditor*, the authorised person or guardian will need authority to grant the discharge, and the relevant interlocutor will require to be registered. The discharge will run in the name of the authorised person or guardian.[4]

---

1 The Keeper is not prepared to accept registration of the interlocutor in advance of the disposition: see *Briefing Note* para 2.3. It is not clear that this practice is justified by the 2000 Act, but the subject will not be explored further here. In practice, of course, conveyancers will normally wish to register contemporaneously.

2 See pp 107–108 above.

3 Paragraphs 7 and 8.

4 There is a style in the *Briefing Note* at para 8.

PART V

TABLES

CUMULATIVE TABLE OF APPEALS 2002

This lists all cases digested in *Conveyancing 1999* and subsequent annual volumes in respect of which an appeal was subsequently heard, and gives the result of the appeal.

Burnett's Tr v Grainger
2000 SLT (Sh Ct) 116 (2000 Case (21)) *rev* 2002 SLT 699 (IH) (2002 Case (19))

Caledonian Heritable Ltd v Canyon Investments Ltd
2001 GWD 1-62 (OH) (2000 Case (69)) *rev* 2002 GWD 5-149 (IH) (2002 Case (61)).

Cheltenham & Gloucester plc v Sun Alliance and London Insurance plc
2001 SLT 347 (OH) (2000 Case (63)) *rev* 2001 SLT 1151 (IH) (2001 Case (73))

Conway v Glasgow City Council
1999 SCLR 248, 1999 Hous LR 20 (Sh Ct) *rev* 1999 SLT (Sh Ct) 102, 1999 SCLR 1058, 1999 Hous LR 67 (1999 Case (44)) *rev* 2001 SLT 1472, 2001 SCLR 546 (IH) (2001 Case (51))

Grampian Joint Police Board v Pearson
2000 SLT 90 (OH) (2000 Case (18)) *affd* 2001 SC 772, 2001 SLT 734 (IH) (2001 Case (17))

Inverness Seafield Co Ltd v Mackintosh
1999 GWD 31-1497 (OH) (1999 Case (19)) *rev* 2001 SC 406, 2001 SLT 118 (IH) (2000 Case (13))

Kaur v Singh (No 2)
1999 Hous LR 76, 2000 SCLR 187, 2000 SLT 1324 (OH) (1999 Case (34)) *affd* 2000 SLT 1323, 2000 SCLR 944 (IH) (2000 Case (26))

Minevco Ltd v Barratt Southern Ltd
1999 GWD 5-266 (OH) (1999 Case (41)) *affd* 2000 SLT 790 (IH) (2000 Case (36))

Robertson v Fife Council
2000 SLT 1226 (OH) (2000 Case (84)) *affd* 2001 SLT 708 (IH) (2001 Case (82)) *rev* 2002 SLT 951 (HL) (2002 Case (69))

Souter v Kennedy
Perth Sheriff Court, 23 July 1999 (unreported) (1999 Case (69)) *rev* 20 March 2001 (unreported) (IH) (2001 Case (81))

Spence v W & R Murray (Alford) Ltd
2001 GWD 7-265 (Sh Ct) (2001 Case (9)) *affd* 2002 SLT 918 (IH) (2002 Case (1))

TABLE OF CASES DIGESTED IN 2001 BUT REPORTED IN 2002

A number of cases which were digested in *Conveyancing 2001* but were at that time unreported have been reported since. A number of other cases have been reported in an additional series of reports. For the convenience of those using the 2001 volume all the cases in question are listed below, together with a complete list of citations.

Bank of Scotland v Fuller Peiser
2002 SLT 574, 2002 SCLR 255 (OH)

Barry v Sutherland
2002 SLT 413, 2002 SCLR 427 (OH)

Bass Brewers Ltd v Independent Insurance Co Ltd
2002 SC 67, 2002 SLT 512 (IH)

Bogie v The Forestry Commission
2002 SCLR 278 (OH)

Gardiner v Jacques Vert plc
2002 SLT 928 (IH)

Howgate Shopping Centre Ltd v GLS 164 Ltd and Pinwise Ltd
2002 SLT 820 (OH)

Mearns v Glasgow City Council
2002 SLT (Sh Ct) 49, 2002 Hous LR 130

Newcastle Building Society v Paterson, Robertson & Graham
2001 SC 734, 2002 SLT 747, 2001 SCLR 737 (OH)

Sutherland v Barry
2002 SLT 418 (OH)

Tait (G W) & Sons v Taylor
2002 SLT 1285, 2002 SCLR 213 (OH)

GLASGOW
Departmental
Libraries
UNIVERSITY